You Can Make
a Difference

You Can Make a Difference

A TEACHER'S GUIDE TO POLITICAL ACTION

Barbara Keresty
Susan O'Leary
Dale Wortley

HEINEMANN
PORTSMOUTH, NH

Heinemann
A division of Reed Elsevier Inc.
361 Hanover Street
Portsmouth, NH 03801-3912

Offices and agents throughout the world

Library of Congress Cataloging-in-Publication Data
Keresty, Barbara.
    You can make a difference : a teacher's guide to political action
 / Barbara Keresty, Susan O'Leary, Dale Wortley.
      p. cm.
    Includes bibliographical references (p. 87).
    ISBN 0-325-00018-2 (alk. paper)
    1. Teachers—United States—Political Activity. I. O'Leary,
Susan, 1950– . II. Wortley, Dale. III. Title.
LB2844.1.P6.K47 1998
371.14'14—dc21   98-10410
                                                                          CIP

Editor: Lois Bridges
Production: Melissa L. Inglis
Cover design: Barbara Werden
Manufacturing: Courtney Ordway

Wisconsin State Journal photo by Roger Turner

Printed in the United States of America on acid-free paper
02 01 00 99 98 DA 1 2 3 4 5

Contents

v

APPENDIXES

Foreword

THIS IS A PARTICULARLY TIMELY BOOK. AMERICAN EDUCATION, especially public education, is the subject of a disinformation campaign—a campaign that seems to be undermining public confidence in public schools (Matthews 1996). The interested reader might turn to *The Manufactured Crisis* by David Berliner and Bruce Biddle for a detailed, scholarly analysis of achievement trends and how the actual achievement patterns have been distorted or misrepresented by government agencies, legislators, lobbyists, and the media. Alternatively, Gerald Bracey's book, *Setting the Record Straight*, offers a more casual treatment, in a question/answer format, of a broader range of misconceptions about American education and American teachers. Both books offer stark evidence of the scope of the disinformation campaign and both offer evidence that contradicts many commonly held and frequently asserted educational "facts." Because American education is under attack and because it seems as if the national leadership of our teacher unions are, at times, too distant from the realities of classrooms and school buildings, especially elementary classrooms, I think teachers need to become more *political* and more often take a proactive stance to protect gains that have been made and to protect programs of promise. For example, in Michigan, Oregon, and Wisconsin, teachers, working with their unions, have been able to advance educational goals that benefit children, their families, and teachers.

Public and Professional Confidence in Education

I worry that the massive disinformation campaign—the campaign that seems to have convinced the public that reading achievement has declined, perhaps dramatically, when achievement actually continues its long, slow creep upward—is beginning to have a negative impact on professional confidence. I worry that we have begun to believe what we read in the papers and hear on television "news" programs and on talk radio shows rather than what we see when we enter our schools and our classrooms. I worry about a "crisis of confidence" in the profession because when we no longer believe in our efforts, our work toward more effective literacy instruction will, inevitably, slacken.

I also worry because the campaign to undermine public confidence in education is well organized (Berliner 1997; Spring 1997). It involves disseminating disinformation both nationally and locally and fostering local distrust of both teachers and school administrators and the decisions they make. The central issue that led to the writing of this guide to political action, *You Can Make a Difference,* was a school district's proposal to substantially reduce funding for support of a local Reading Recovery program. In this case, no outside forces advocated this proposal—a shift in budget priorities sat at the base of the decision. But elsewhere there have been organized assaults, including massive disinformation dissemination, on the Reading Recovery effort, including legislative proposals to disallow public funding. If a program as well researched and as successful as Reading Recovery can come under such intensive assault, then literally any educational effort is vulnerable.

Unions, Teachers, and Political Activity

Teachers, especially, need to create more viable political movements. Perhaps we all must work harder to shift the attention of national leaders of teacher unions toward the things that really matter in teaching. The failures of both the National Education Association and the American Federation of Teachers recently to support teachers in the face of legislative actions that undermine local autonomy and professional decision-making about appropriate reading instruction (e.g., AB 1086 in California and HR2614 in the

U.S. Congress) are worrisome. If the national leaders of both unions are falling out of touch with the local members, that is a cause for concern, but also a reason for initiating political action within those organizations to ensure they continue their long history of advocating for both teachers and pupils. Unions aren't just about local contracts and building grievances—state and national teacher unions are powerful political action organizations that shape legislative activity.

Teachers must make better use of their unions' political expertise and political clout. For instance, teachers might expect their unions to create the sort of electronic mail communications that would allow an efficient and easy flow of information among the membership and between the membership and the union leadership. Our current research on educational policymaking in four states suggests, however, that such systems are not typically available. In contrast, the CATEnet system of the California Association of Teachers of English and that of the California Literacy Educators offer literacy educators statewide access to both local and national issues and information. It was these systems that fostered the political resistance to the "stealth standards" movement in California. Unfortunately, the teachers that participated in these networks found themselves in opposition to their own unions—this resulted from the failure of the union leadership to actively analyze legislative proposals and to actively access the expertise and stances of their members.

Political Shifts and Administrator Shuffles

Teachers need to be politically active locally as well. The mobility of administrators is well documented, especially those administrators in the most prominent policy-making positions: superintendents, assistant superintendents, and directors. This constant shuffling of top administrators means that often school policies shift as administrators shift (Johnston, Allington, Guice, and Brooks, in press). In contrast, most teachers begin and end their careers in the same district. Thus, it is the classroom teacher who is most likely to remain at the scene of any educational reform effort—remain in the classroom, in the school, in the district where any reform is proposed or initiated. Too often before a given reform is fully implemented the administrator who proposed and championed the reform has left the position and, typically, left the district. But the teachers who have been working to implement the reform remain.

This stability of teachers in schools and districts seems a good reason for teachers to be deeply involved in reform decisions. In fact, there are other reasons as well. Our recent longitudinal study of teacher change—in districts implementing literature-based instruction—documented the positive effects of more decentralized decision-making. When districts involved teachers in the decision to shift to literature-based instruction the implementation process was more actively supported by teachers such that more substantive and more enduring change was observed. In addition, achievement rose in the decentralized districts while it declined in the districts where decisions were largely centralized and where teachers were not involved in the reform decisions and where few were champions of the reform effort (Johnston, Allington, Guice, and Brooks, in press).

Unfortunately, the historical rise of the large, bureaucratic school system has meant that in too many districts teachers are not much involved in the decisions to implement reform activities. The much more recent emphasis on state- and federally-initiated top-down reforms has shifted decision-making even further from the classroom. The shifting politics at both the state and national levels produce an instability similar to, but more far-reaching, than the administrative mobility noted above (Chrispeels 1997). But as education becomes more politicized and it is becoming increasingly so, teachers must also become more politically astute and more politically involved.

Teachers too often become politically active only when some truly useful educational effort is threatened, as in the story presented in this book where involvement was spurred by a centralized administrative decision to abandon a successful reform initiative in the face of budget difficulties. Fortunately, the campaign was successful. But I think we can expect more frequent questions about our programs generally and about innovative programs specifically. The questions will come not just from those who would work to undermine public confidence in public education but from concerned parents and citizens as we attempt to develop the schools we need for the new demands of a more technological society.

The Grammar of Schooling

Tyack and Cuban (1995) trace the ebb and flow of educational reform activity in American schools across the last century. They suggest that there is a "grammar of schooling" that operates very much like the grammar of language—in ways that most persons are not conscious of and could not explain. This grammar of school develops from our experience with schools and includes the notion of a "real school." Real schools, for instance, have separate subjects, offer tests in each of those subjects, give grades, send home report cards and homework worksheets, assign book reports and chapter questions, have the teacher in front of the room with children at desks in rows not speaking until called upon, and so on. They argue that whenever reform efforts too seriously violate the grammar of schools that most people hold near and dear, objections arise. These objections can become outright resistance movements when the school response is perceived as fuzzy or condescending.

If we want to hold on to the progress we make in changing schools, in improving instructional programs, then we must expect resistance when we reform in ways that violate the grammar of schooling held by the public. A most important sort of political activity for teachers is the proactive dissemination of information, including achievement information, about the reforms we have implemented. Lobbyists talk of "message discipline" or making sure that every caller or letter writer emphasizes the same theme or themes. I think we might learn something from this.

Too often, in my experience, our "lobbying" efforts in support of a particular change or innovation take on a sort of scattershot image with no message discipline. Every proponent offers their reasons for support, too often based primarily in preference or anecdote. But often "data" are demanded, not warm and cozy teacher stories or teacher testimonials (although testimonials from parents and students can be powerful when coupled with data, as this book demonstrates). Most advocacy efforts, I believe, would be more successful with better data and with greater message discipline. But accomplishing both will require organization and effort.

California and Invented Spelling as an Illustrative Case

We may see how introducing "invented spelling" in kindergarten and first grade has produced a remarkable shift in the development of literacy but the grammar of schooling calls for accuracy, red ink and corrections, and, perhaps, copying from the board. We might show parents how invented spelling activity enhances the development of phonemic awareness and understanding of the alphabetic principle, but we have rarely done this. We might demonstrate that children are still learning conventional spellings at least as well as has been the case historically, but often we don't.

Now, this may seem hardly a political case, but consider that "inventive spelling" is one of the topics now legislatively banned from professional development sessions in California. Consider the number of states now reintroducing a spelling basal and putting spelling grades back on report cards. The grammar of schooling produces a powerful image of how spelling is done in real schools. With little organized, supportive, political activism from teachers, one of the most powerful pedagogical advances of this century was, literally, banned from Bakersfield to Berkeley. But before it was banned statewide, there were incidences of similar local actions that put invented spelling on the action agenda and, ultimately, led to the reintroduction of the traditional, if ineffective, weekly spelling test. With no effective political activity and little, if any, proactive, preventive planning, teachers saw the power of the public "grammar of schooling."

Tip O'Neil, the longstanding Speaker of the U.S. House of Representatives said, "All politics are local." Keep this in mind as you read this primer on becoming more political. Keep also in mind my argument for greater teacher involvement in the local politics of education, especially those decisions about curriculum and instruction. Teachers can be a powerful political force as the authors demonstrate in this case study. But, first, teachers must become more political—more proactively political. This book can help you in this process.

Richard L. Allington

References

Allington, R. L., and H. Woodside-Jiron. 1997. *Adequacy of a Program of Research and of a "Research Synthesis" in Shaping Educational Policy*. No. 1.15. Albany, NY: National Research Center on English Learning and Achievement, State University of New York at Albany.

Berliner, D. C. 1997. "Educational Psychology Meets the Christian Right: Differing Views of Children, Schooling, Teaching, and Learning." *Teachers College Record* 98: 381–416.

Berliner, D. C., and B. J. Biddle. 1996. *The Manufactured Crisis: Myths, Fraud, and the Attack on America's Public Schools*. White Plains, NY: Longman.

Bracey, G. W. 1997. *Setting the Record Straight: Responses to Misconceptions About Public Education in the United States*. Alexandria, VA: Association for Supervision and Curriculum Development.

Chrispeels, J. H. 1997. "Educational Policy Implementation in a Shifting Political Climate: The California Experience." *American Educational Research Journal* 34: 453–481.

Johnston, P. A., R. L. Allington, S. Guice, and G. Brooks. In press. "Why Should Teachers Change?" *Peabody Journal of Education.*

Matthews, D. 1996. *Is There a Public for the Public Schools?* Dayton, OH: Kettering Foundation.

Spring, J. 1997. *Political Agendas for Education: From the Christian Coalition to the Green Party.* Mahwah, NJ: Lawrence Erlbaum.

Tyack, D., and L. Cuban. 1995. *Tinkering Toward Utopia: A Century of Public School Reform.* Cambridge, MA: Harvard University Press.

Acknowledgments

A BOOK COMES INTO BEING THROUGH THE EFFORT OF MANY. Our book was shaped by our learning from others. Marie Clay's thoughtful observations of developing readers led to her powerful theory of reading. We thank her for enriching our lives and giving us the tools to help children reach their highest potential.

Regie Routman's book *Literacy at the Crossroads* inspired our book. Regie continued to inspire us as she graciously read our manuscript and provided helpful feedback. Richard Allington kindly gave his time to read the book and write its foreword. We found his positive response most rewarding.

John Matthews, the Executive Director of our teachers' union, Madison Teachers Incorporated, taught us about political action, about staying involved, and defending with passion what you believe in. We are privileged to work with and continue to learn from someone who has been called the greatest negotiator in Wisconsin's labor history.

We wish to thank all those who so willingly gave their time and expertise during the course of the writing of this book. We thank Lois Bridges, our editor at Heinemann, who, when she heard our presentation at the Ohio Reading Recovery Conference in February 1997, insisted, "There's a book here!" Besides gaining an editor with foresight, we've gained a friend. Tom Johnson read our manuscript with the insight and dedication of an editor. He helped immensely to tighten and reorganize early drafts. Chris Weber, Mary Michal, Jim Roseberry, Francie Sullivan, and Nan Brien all offered helpful comments in their reading of various stages of our manuscript. We thank them for their interest and time.

We offer our separate thanks as well.

From Barbara Keresty: My husband, Tom Johnson, a skillful writer with a fine ear for the English language, provided much needed assistance with early edits. Tom also endured numerous early morning and late night phone calls with colleagues during my involvement with political action activities. Tom's mother, Modeste Johnson, made helpful suggestions. Her own background as a secondary teacher of English and as one of only two women high school principals in the State of Wisconsin in the early 1960s contributed a unique perspective.

My parents, Anna and William Paes, as always, constantly encouraged me as I stepped into yet another challenging endeavor. My sisters, Shirley Glavan and Patricia Winterburn, and my brother Terry Keresty, offered support in countless ways as they so often do. My friend, Nancy Heberlein, who has helped me meet deadlines on various projects over the years, came through once more with hours of typing.

Thank you to Patty Schenk for her early reading and edits to Chapter 2. Colleagues Jody Gilbertson and Kari Snyder deserve a special thank you for their technical assistance. I thank Kathy Collins and Susan Yapp for listening to me and giving me advice that I actually took.

From Susan O'Leary: I could not have made my contribution to our book without the kind patience and encouragement of my family: my husband, Jim Roseberry, and our children, Nate, Nora, and Tom O'Leary-Roseberry. They helped me meet tight deadlines by taking over my responsibilities in our home, luring me away on necessary bike rides, and buying me chocolate. Nora and Sister Theresa Panther both allowed me the time and mind to write by taking care of Tom.

Mary Thompson became a part of this book through many long distance phone calls; I have relied on her sense of humor for most of my life. Chuck Curtis, once again, offered generous advice.

Books evolve from a specific time and place. My contribution to our book is grounded in my involvement in two communities: Franklin Elementary School and the Madison Snowflower Sangha. I thank the members of both communities for all they have given to me.

I feel fortunate that writing this book gave me the opportunity to open books by Martin Luther King, Jr. His words and courage remain an inspiration. I am grateful that Thich Nhat Hanh and Chân Không, through their writing and by their example, have been a part of my life for years. I thank them for being my teachers.

Finally, to end at the beginning, I thank my parents, Gar and Ginger O'Leary. I think my father would have been pleased with the tone and purpose of this book. My mother, as always, supports me with generosity and love. I hope that my children when grown feel as lucky to have had me for a mother as I feel to be my parents' daughter.

From Dale Wortley: I am keenly aware of the debt of gratitude owed to so many colleagues, parents, and other community members, all of whom played a vital role in this story. Over a period of eight years, so many gave their precious time and energy to fight the good fight for children that I cannot begin to name individuals. You know who you are, and I am thankful to each and every one of you. Without you this story would not exist. I hope the story will be meaningful and useful to others facing political dilemmas in their own schools.

In closing, the three of us thank, most importantly, the Madison Reading Recovery teachers for never giving up.

Introduction

As I left my car in a school parking lot, heading for an after school class, I met another Reading Recovery teacher. We had not really known each other until we became involved in a group working to save the Reading Recovery program in our Madison, Wisconsin schools. As we walked in one of the first spring rains, the teacher started telling me how uncharacteristic it had been for her to come to a meeting of teachers at my house. In a quiet voice, she continued. She had never done anything like this before. As a result of going to the meeting, she then attended a school board meeting and was glad she had. For this teacher, as for many others, becoming politically active was a huge step in a brand new direction. Having had this experience, this teacher might well get involved in fighting for other causes in which she believes. In a small way, our actions to save Reading Recovery changed her life and her sense of self. In organizing politically, you may have a much bigger effect on the world than you know.

IN THE SPRING OF 1996, THE BOARD OF EDUCATION OF THE Madison Metropolitan School District considered cutting several programs to meet state-mandated spending cuts. One of the programs they targeted to cut in half and possibly eliminate was the Reading Recovery program. Reading Recovery teachers and the parents of the participating children came together and convinced the board of education and the superintendent not to cut our program.

You Can Make a Difference: A Teacher's Guide to Political Action tells the story of what we did and how we did it. Our experiences provide a model for others who need to organize politically.

Acting at first simply from strong conviction—as teachers, we had witnessed again and again how Reading Recovery changes children's lives—we learned in those months much about how to be political and to work together effectively. We want to share what we learned with others interested in becoming advocates for education.

You Can Make a Difference is written as a primer, with clear, specific steps for undertaking political action for education at a local level. This book is intended for all believers in public education: teachers, parents, union members, administrators, curriculum coordinators, those involved in the politics of reading, and, of course, Reading Recovery teachers.

We would have had no program to save if Dale Wortley and members of the Madison Metropolitan School District's Reading Needs Project had not, more than ten years earlier, worked hard to bring Reading Recovery to the Madison schools. So we begin our story at its roots, starting not with how to save a program, but with how to create or bring a program in which you believe to your school.

Chapter 1 details specific steps for the initiation and successful implementation of a program. It describes how to research a solution; gain the support of administrators, other teachers, and board members; develop an evaluation plan; and secure funding. With the program in place, you can ensure its longevity by building a base of support, reaching out to other programs, continuing to evaluate your program's effectiveness, and advocating for your program.

Even after all that work, your program can still be threatened. Chapter 2 outlines specific steps to take in organizing to defend a program: rallying teachers, appearing at school board meetings, establishing connections with the media, and creating relationships with the board.

In Chapter 3, we discuss further aspects of thinking and acting politically: learning from other political leaders, creating a focus, providing leadership, speaking publicly, getting sustenance from doing it because it's the right thing to do, and, an important part of acting politically, taking care of yourself.

Finding one narrative voice for the three writers who worked on different aspects of our political action campaign has had its difficulties. Dale Wortley is a Reading Recovery teacher-leader who helped bring the Reading Recovery program to the Madison schools. Barb Keresty and Susan O'Leary are Reading Recovery teachers who led the campaign that saved the Reading Recovery program when cuts threatened its existence. In the first chapter, which focuses on Dale's work, we use *I* for her narrative voice. In Chapters 2 and 3, which describe the work Barb and Susan led, we usually use *we*. At times, however, we refer to *Barb and Susan* for clarity.

We live in a time when public education is under attack in the United States. The state-mandated limit on local education spending in Wisconsin made our program subject to cuts.

Sadly, a strong public education system is only rarely perceived as the foundation for democracy and the social fabric that binds us all together. Indeed, democracy is often equated with measures to cut more taxes. We hope that *You Can Make a Difference* will also be an impetus to shift how we think and how we speak about education in a democracy. We will be most pleased if the ideas we present help others to advocate at a state and a national level, as well as on a local level.

Finally, we assume that your convictions have inspired you to act politically, rather than a need for something else to do in this busy world. You may not even *want* to take on political action, but you feel compelled to speak up for what you believe is right. *You Can Make a Difference* is written to help you learn quickly what to do, how to be effective as you become involved politically, and how to maintain some balance as battles intensify. We hope it gives you courage and help along the way.

Good luck!

1

How to Get a Program

How It All Began

Justin came from a family with a history of drug and alcohol abuse. Learning was difficult for him, and it was suspected he suffered from fetal alcohol syndrome. Because Justin was not learning to read along with the other students in the class, his teacher Ann sought extra help for him. Without realizing it, in trying to get help for Justin, Ann played a key role in changing how reading was taught to struggling Madison first graders districtwide. The search for an answer for Ann was what eventually brought Reading Recovery to Madison.

In fact, change typically happens at a grassroots level in education because of situations just like Justin's. A student isn't learning, and his teacher tries to find help for him. A school suddenly starts to have more discipline problems, and the staff wants to find a more effective solution. A teacher reads a professional book over the summer and returns to school fired up by new ideas. Parents want after-school programs for their children and form a group to press for them.

In this chapter we outline what to do when you have that new idea. We tell the story of how Dale Wortley and other members of the Reading Needs Project in the Madison schools researched, planned, and advocated until Reading Recovery was initiated, implemented, and institutionalized as a program in the Madison Metropolitan School District. Every situation is different, but we believe our experience will serve as an example of how to get a new program started within a school system.

The chapter is divided into two sections. The first, Initiating a New

Program, outlines seeing the need; recognizing that you are involved in change; researching the program; being aware of how it meshes with local goals and standards; gaining district support; finding funding; and creating an evaluation plan.

However, a program is not secured because it has been launched. The second part of the chapter, Implementing and Institutionalizing the Program, explains how to maintain your new project by expanding your base of support; reaching out to other programs in your district; having a long-term plan; and continuing to advocate.

Initiating a New Program

See the Need

A new program won't be successful unless all parties recognize and agree to the need for it. The first step in getting a new program therefore begins with seeing and clarifying that need. In clarifying it, you may find that your understanding of the need changes.

In the late 1970s, a Madison philanthropist donated thousands of dollars to the school district to hire reading specialists to test low-achieving readers, and to provide diagnostic reports of the results for classroom teachers. This was the beginning of a Madison Metropolitan School District program called the Reading Needs Project.

Though the diagnostic testing helped to pinpoint who needed help and how much help, it wasn't long before everyone recognized that this was just the start of something big. Finding out *who* needed help didn't make them better readers. The test results begged for translation into informed instruction—how could we best teach the low-achieving students so that they would catch up with their peers? The need for informed instruction in turn begged for staff development on researched best practices; if we were really going to focus on these students, we wanted teachers using the best techniques. The impetus, the funding, and the administrative support for improving children's reading were all there. The Reading Needs Project quickly evolved from pure testing to one-year residencies for three reading specialists in different Madison elementary schools.

It was an exciting time. We taught after-school classes on reading instruction to teachers at our resident schools, in the process helping them develop a schoolwide philosophy about the teaching of reading. We went into classrooms and demonstrated techniques for teaching reading in small groups and to the entire class. Each Friday the administrator of curriculum and instruction and the reading specialists met to evaluate the progress of the program. We shared successes and frustrations, and through our discussions we defined common goals for improving reading instruction in Madison.

It was as the reading specialist at her school that year that Dale Wortley worked in Ann's classroom. Dale's account, which follows, tells of her work with Justin and its far-reaching ramifications.

Because Justin was the student that Ann was most concerned about helping, I began working individually with him. I was also at this time just discovering research by Marie Clay, the creator of Reading Recovery. Her writings had convinced me that a small number of students having difficulty getting started in reading and writing absolutely required one-on-one tutoring to learn to read.

Justin seemed like the perfect candidate with whom to try the procedures in Clay's (1983) *The Early Detection of Reading Difficulties*. But it soon became apparent to me that while Clay's research had all the proof of a successful pudding, her handbook was not, and is not, a cookbook that can be successfully followed without in-depth study guided by a knowledgeable, trained instructor. For example, I diligently tried the procedures and techniques suggested in Clay's book to help children who have a hard time remembering and learning letters and words. Unfortunately, my efforts did not help Justin improve significantly in these areas. I lacked the understanding required to meet his particular needs.

We needed an accelerative one-on-one intervention for the lowest-achieving beginning readers to complement the Reading Needs Project. The testing and staff development had shown us the one important remaining need: finding a way to teach the first graders who were not learning to read.

All of the research from New Zealand and Columbus, Ohio, on the Reading Recovery program convinced me that this program, with its statistically verified results, provided the best answer. I felt that since we knew the program existed, we had a moral obligation to provide instruction in a method for which there was proven success. I had tried to apply the theory in working one-on-one with Justin, but realized I could not implement the technique successfully without training. I had seen a need and found what I thought was an answer for it. Now I would spend a year and a half learning how long bringing about a change can take.

Recognize You Are Involved in Change

I'm an avid cartoon reader. I just plain enjoy a good cartoon. They wow me by the complexity of the message that can be communicated in a simple picture and a minimum of words. When I encounter one that I feel is exceptionally well done and that strikes an immediate and loud chord, I am not hesitant to share it.

One of my all-time favorite cartoons is from the *New Yorker*. This particular cartoon pictures a benevolent-looking, bearded king, high up on a balcony clothed in velvet, ermine, and crown, and to the throng of expressionless people below he is saying, with a kind smile on his face: "It is my wish that this be the most educated country in the world, and toward that end I hereby ordain that each and every one of my people be given a diploma."

The king just didn't get it; change is a *process*, not a proclamation. This understanding is primary in starting a new program. A change in the status quo is the result of a carefully orchestrated plan for initiation and implementation over a long period of time. When you are starting out, you need to realize that affecting change will probably take longer than you expect or want, and plan accordingly.

Schools are organized in part by tradition and in part by laws, regulations, and contracts. A new idea will not be implemented just because it is good. In bringing a new program to your district, keep remembering that you are involved in change. A new idea must become, for a while, a process.

Part of being involved with change is having a well thought-out plan. No matter how excellent, an idea in and of itself is not enough. Be prepared for the long haul of working through stages of initiating a plan, implementing the new program, and institutionalizing the program. I spent approximately two years just laying the groundwork to initiate the Reading Recovery program for our district before going to Ohio State for a year of intensive training as a teacher-leader in the program. We are currently going into our tenth year; now that's a good track record for longevity in educational programming!

Become Very Knowledgeable About the Program You Want to Initiate. It is not enough to come back from a conference or a workshop presentation fired up by a particular speaker or to be captivated by something you've read that seems to make a lot of sense. While these experiences may plant a seed for nurturing thought, there is still a lot more investigating and learning required. You need to delve deeply, explore thoroughly, and enlist support for your project.

My introduction to Clay's Reading Recovery program was at an International Reading Association convention. I returned to my school district anxious to share with the other reading specialists what I had learned. I talked at our Friday meetings about what I understood of the program and its results.

My colleagues quickly became interested, and together we searched and studied the literature and research available on the program. (Be wary if a literature search turns up very little or nothing at all on a program. It may not be worth your time and energy.) We poured over my new copy of Clay's book, *The Early Detection of Reading Difficulties*. We read as many articles as we could find in professional journals and continued to discuss our discoveries at the Friday meetings in order build group knowledge. One of the other reading specialists gave an inservice, based on Clay's work on assessment, for special education teachers. We all now saw the power of and wanted to know more about Clay's research.

A crucial step in securing district support for a new program, then, is gaining interest and support from colleagues with whom you work most closely.

Now that we had a background knowledge of Reading Recovery, we moved to the next step—locating and telephoning people and districts who were involved in a Reading Recovery program. The program looked fantastic in articles, but what did teachers think in districts that had actually implemented it? There were few Reading Recovery programs in the United States at that point, but we called anywhere we could—Austin, Texas; the Ohio elementary schools involved in the Ohio State training; schools in Virginia. Before calling, my colleagues and I came up with a list of specific questions that came from our study and discussions. Where had the districts obtained funding? What were their evaluation results? What had they learned and what advice would they have for someone else?

People in other districts will generally want to be helpful, but they can be more helpful if you can efficiently tell them exactly what it is you want clarified. Don't call without a specific list of questions. Have it in front of you as you speak.

The phone calls confirmed what we had read about Reading Recovery. Districts were excited. They saw clear, accelerated progress with the children in the program. It was reassuring to learn that the program was transferrable from its original pilot site, Columbus, Ohio. If districts in other parts of the country had been equally successful in implementing the program, then surely we could be also.

My supervisor in curriculum and instruction was as excited as I was about the prospect of radically improving reading instruction for struggling children *before* they saw themselves as failing. She was supportive of my travel to The Ohio State University, where the program was already in place, so that I could observe the instruction and continue to ask questions.

My colleagues and I once again developed a protocol of questions to assure that I returned with the information that I most needed to move forward in our quest to have a Reading Recovery program in our district. Now the questions were more specific and related to the nitty-gritty details of teacher training, materials, levels of commitment on the part of the school district and individual schools and teachers, training the trainer of teachers, roles and responsibilities of personnel, and the actual setting up of the training facility.

As part of my visit to Ohio State, I also observed at local elementary schools with Reading Recovery programs. At these schools I saw the program in action and got direct answers and reactions from principals and teachers already involved in Reading Recovery. Visiting sites where Reading Recovery was taught gave me a much deeper understanding of the theory behind the program and of how it was changing students' lives.

To advocate successfully for a new program in the schools, you need to be as knowledgeable as possible about the program. Build on what you know, and keep researching. We began by reading everything available in articles and books. I then interviewed people by telephone and finally visited in person. Each stage of research prepared me for the next. Learn as much as you can about the program you are interested in. Other teachers and administrators will take you much more seriously if you can explain the program clearly—both simply and in detail—and answer their questions.

Be Aware of and Respond to Local Goals and Standards. The next step is to take your research and present it in relation to your district's goals and standards. The new program being introduced to your school system must have specific goals, and its benefits must be presented in ways that catch and compel the attention of the district's decision makers. In the case of Reading Recovery, it was not difficult to align goals and benefits of the program with already existing goals and standards established by the district. The whole language philosophy of teaching and learning how to read and write was at that time, and continues to be, that of our district's language arts program. District administration saw Reading Recovery as aligning with that philosophy. Additionally, our district has always identified meeting the needs of low-achieving readers as a major goal of its reading program. The goals and benefits of a Reading Recovery program are to significantly reduce the numbers of low-achieving readers in a school district. Matches such as this are made in heaven.

In preparing our presentation to an administrative cabinet we were careful to spell out the important connections between the new program and already existing district goals and objectives. Demonstrating this relationship is necessary for gaining approval to start a new program. Arguments against a new idea will fold if the presentation fits perfectly in the district's overall plan. Both the Reading Needs Project and the Reading Recovery program were systemic in nature; that is, they were adopted by the school district as part of an overall effort to increase reading achievement.

You are much more likely to gain approval for your new program if you know your district goals and policies and can connect with them.

Secure Commitment from Your District Administration. Now that you have done your homework and are confident you know what you are talking about, the next step is to identify key administrators to advocate for your program. We each have limited power within a school district and need to develop a power base from which acceptance of our idea can expand.

Things work differently in different districts. In our district the best approach is first to garner administrative support, and then to have administrators take the idea to the board of education. Find out the best way to proceed in your district.

I had to be patient about each bureaucratic hoop that presented itself, demanding that I jump through it. Making connections and scheduling meetings with a hierarchy of administrative personnel and committees take time. Schools have rules, regulations, policies, and protocols that must be respected. The politically active fare better by knowing and working within rather than against the system. By being savvy about the politics of your school district, you will improve your chances of procuring administrative support.

Begin by working with your most immediate supervisor. Respecting the chain of command is a must. Once we had gained the support of our immediate supervisor for the idea of bringing Reading Recovery to Madison, she then arranged meetings with key administrative cabinets who would ultimately have to approve or disapprove our final proposal. Before you meet with higher-level administration, identify implementation issues such as finding funding for human and material resources; long-range planning for stages of implementation; and training needs. Work with your immediate supervisor to target administrators or administrative committees that will be critical for the program's implementation.

As you go higher into administration with your idea, the kinds of questions you are asked may change. This stage gives you a new set of questions to think about, a way of framing the issue of which you probably were not aware in your first excitement about the program. Listen closely to administrators' implementation concerns because cost and results are what they need to look at. Be able to describe your program idea *simply* in terms of what it will cost and what the district will get for its money, and *in detail* in terms of factors like teacher allocations, training expenses, teaching materials, clerical assistance, office materials, printing, and program evaluation materials and services. Remember to explain costs and benefits in terms of how the program fits in with the district philosophy and goals.

A high level of commitment to a program requires a high level of knowledge about the program, and we were asking for a high level of commitment from administration. We owed it to our administrators to provide the information they needed in order to give us their support.

Be Realistic and Creative in Looking for Funding. In *No Quick Fix,* Richard Allington (1995) decries the lack of long-term planning by schools for funding improvements and restructuring efforts to benefit children. Take heed of his advice. You need to have a handle on both immediate and future funding needs related to the program you want. Be specific and detailed in the program needs, and identify potential sources of funding for them. People often look first for "soft" monies or short-term grants. Some programs can start or operate under those circumstances. However, you need to consider seriously whether your program will be able to flourish and survive with this kind of funding. If you are beginning with a grant, from the first stages of implementation look for more secure sources of funds.

We investigated all sources we could think of—district funding, grants, Title monies, and special school-based funds set aside for minority student achievement. Every district and community will have its own variety of funding sources. Your immediate supervisor should understand how your district's funding and budget work and be able to help you research funding. You might also ask her or him to call a meeting for you with your district's department of budget and accounting to ask budget questions. Again, think out your questions before you go. In looking for funding, you will be researching in much the same way you did when you first looked into your program. Read. Make phone calls. Find out as much as you can.

Have an Evaluation Plan in Place. Administrators and the board of education will take you much more seriously if you have an evaluation plan to offer along with your proposal for implementation. The plan needs to be able to produce hard data to show the results of your program. Testimonials will show a need or an important effect, but administrators, boards of education, and parents are much more comfortable with hard data to account for the success of a program. In our district, administrative goals demand accountability if a program is to be recognized as more than educational rhetoric. One reason the Reading Recovery program appeals to administrators, board members, classroom teachers, and parents is the high level of accountability that is automatically built into the program—daily computing of a child's oral reading accuracy; weekly charting of a child's progress in book levels and in the words the child can write; grade level requirements in both reading and writing before a child can test out of the program; districtwide analysis of number of days children are in the program; aggregation of data according to economic status, ethnicity, and gender; and follow-up studies with former Reading Recovery students when they take the Wisconsin Third Grade Reading Test.

Most school districts have their own approach to evaluation. Rely on the expertise of the person in your district who is responsible for evaluation of district achievement. With him or her, come up with an evaluation plan that will test the results of your program. You will look much more credible if an independent expert helped to create your evaluation plan.

Implementing and Institutionalizing the Program

Educational programs have a history of being short-lived. A new interest, a new phase, a new need will come along and the district will move on to something else. Initiating a program is not the hardest part of the process. The greater challenge lies in proper implementation, followed by institutionalization of a program. Both are intrinsic to long-term success.

Expand the Support Base

Now that the administration and the board have given the green light to your new program and have assured the necessary budget, you must establish district and school staff commitment and parent involvement. This critical audience needs to know details about the program, how it works within the school environment and how it will benefit the children. Developing cooperation among all involved helps ensure success. Classroom teachers and parents have been the lifesavers of both the Reading Needs Project and the Reading Recovery program in times of district budget debates over the years. Keep both groups well informed.

Once we were ready to go forward with implementing Reading Recovery, I made myself available whenever possible to do presentations about the program to interested audiences. After my trip to Ohio, where I had taken lots of photos, I made slide presentations to school staffs to raise interest levels. Classroom teachers and principals liked being given the opportunity to *see* how the program would work. We also designed and disseminated a succinct, informative pamphlet describing the Reading Recovery program and answering questions about the program. We left these with the audience for future reference. Because of these meetings, before the program became operational in a school, the staff had a clear picture of what to expect and not to expect. I made this same kind of presentation at more than fifteen parent association meetings. When you speak to parent groups, it is important to speak in lay terms. You could actually lose parent support by presenting your program primarily in educational jargon.

Once the program was in place, I wrote articles about Reading Recovery that were published in both district-level and school-level newsletters that went home to parents. This publicity raised awareness of the program and its effect across the district. Keeping a new program visible and in a positive light can bolster its survival as well as promote its expansion.

I earned my fifteen minutes of fame when I was interviewed on local television about the value and results of Reading Recovery. Making the general community aware of a program that is working positively for kids can pay dividends later, especially at budget time.

As educational budgets get tighter and tighter, you also need to be able to show the exact effect of your program. Getting on agendas at principals' meetings and board of education meetings also helps build commitment among the leadership. In subsequent years presentations can show longitudinal data for your program to ensure continued support. One of the most powerful factors contributing to the longevity of the Reading Recovery program in our district is the follow-up data we have been able to provide. The district has been able to see a return on its investment.

Reach Out to and Collaborate with Other Programs in Your District

In bringing about change, you will meet resistance. Expect this, and as you develop a response, you will often find that the importance of and need for your program have been clarified. In meeting resistance, listen for the value in programs already in place and how you can work together.

As the Reading Recovery program began to be introduced in our district, some district staff were understandably leery of infringement on their domains. This issue had to be respectfully addressed. For example, because Reading Recovery and Title I programs basically serve the same population, there were concerns and feelings of competitiveness that initially caused disharmony between the two programs. This was a problem we had neglected to anticipate, so we present our mistakes in the hope that you will be able to learn from them.

It took sensitive interaction during the first few years of implementation to bring the two programs comfortably together in the partnership that had always been envisioned but that we had neglected to build into the initiation phase. We reached a partnership by conscious, systematic inclusion of Title I staff in all relevant aspects of the Reading Recovery program (e.g., testing, student selection, evaluation), as well as sharing materials and practices. Title I teachers were also trained in Reading Recovery, creating natural links between the two programs. We regretted that, through oversight, we had not collaborated from the beginning. Our advice is to be open, inclusive, and willing to exchange information with groups or programs with which your program intersects.

After overcoming our growing pains, Reading Recovery and Title I have become a mean teaching machine. They complement each other's efforts to help children succeed. When you are starting a new program, never neglect the power of collaboration with all the good and the strong forces that already exist in your district. Cooperation with existing programs will help guarantee your success.

Change within an educational system is a complex process, and new programs are not easily or automatically maintained. Long-term tending is required for institutionalizing a program. Constant efforts, year after year, are necessary for a program to be understood and viewed as an educational opportunity without which children's level of achievement will be diminished.

Clay (1994) points out that there is a continual need for Reading Recovery to explain itself to new audiences—a major lesson regarding the maintenance of any program. Innovative programs need never-ending political attention if they are to become integrally institutional.

You must continue to provide information and to be willing to start again at the beginning for the administrators and board members of today who are not the same as those of two years ago; for the local journalists who are not the same as those of last year; for the parents and school staffs who represent a different audience from that of the previous year. Recognize that maintaining a program demands continual reeducation for new administrators, board members, media personnel, parents, teachers, and taxpayers.

Have a Long-Term Plan for Full Implementation and Institutionalization

Properly implemented programs based on solid research can greatly benefit a school system. In the case of the Reading Recovery program we developed a plan for full implementation that we determined should take six years.

Make your long-range plan. We determined ours with projections of first graders in the district, average enrollments per class, numbers of students equal to 20 percent of the first-grade population, and numbers of teachers needed to serve this population. Just as when you were advocating for the implementation of your program, estimate costs for the number of teachers needed, supplies, training, and clerical support. Be specific, and make it easy for your district to go ahead with your program.

Never Stop Advocating

The Reading Recovery program has been a part of Madison schools since the 1989–1990 school year. It has changed the lives of over one thousand children, helping them to become successful readers. Before Reading Recovery, these children risked staying at the bottom of their classes, unsure of themselves and their potential.

Because we had a strong plan for securing implementation (and we learned the patience to continue advocating for two years), we have made a difference in our schools and in our community. By following these steps, by staying committed, you can, too.

Our long-term plan has moved forward year by year. Ten years into our program, however, we still have not achieved full implementation. That is a reality of our political situation, where administrative changes in leadership and restructuring can result in a shift in priorities and where local education budgets are capped by state law. Every year we have had to organize for political action at annual budget deliberation time in order to keep Reading Recovery visible to the board, administration, and community in general. As a result, our program has slowly grown.

Still, factors periodically arise that threaten an innovation. When resources are minimal, excellent programs are put in jeopardy. Long-term plans get "shucked" and stepped-up political action is called for. Sean Walmsley, in *No Quick Fix* (Allington and Walmsley 1995), states that good ideas need good politics to help them get initiated, and even better politics to keep them going.

In Chapter 2 we describe how we organized citywide to keep this program we so firmly believed in.

2

How to Keep a Program

IN THE WINTER OF 1996 WE LEARNED THAT OUR READING Recovery program was slated for the spring budget chopping block. This action meant that more than twenty teachers would lose their jobs. But it meant more than that: it meant that close to two hundred children would not get the reading instruction they needed. That number would multiply each passing year. Such a deep cut in the program was a strong signal to us that administration and board support for our program was vanishing. We knew that we had to act.

This chapter highlights the most important steps we took in saving our program: organizing supporters, organizing around a focus, working with our union, developing and maintaining connections with the school board, and developing and maintaining connections with the media. Thanks to the efforts of hundreds of people, the superintendent and the school board chose, in a very tight budget year, to maintain all Reading Recovery positions.

Reading Recovery remains a successful program in the Madison school district because of the continued commitment of many dedicated people. The political action that resulted in our program's salvation is presented here, with strategies and examples of how a successful political action plan, when properly executed, can lead to victory.

Organize Your Most Obvious Supporters

We began by organizing Reading Recovery teachers. At the continuing training session where we first heard about the proposed cuts, we announced a meeting of Reading Recovery teachers at Susan's house. We had no idea what the meeting would be about, but we knew we had an audience right there that we needed to bring together. We could plan for the initial meeting later. Right now we needed to take the risk and call the meeting. (See Appendix A.)

While organizing Reading Recovery teachers was the obvious first step for us, much of what we did could equally apply to organizing parents, students, and other community members. Organizing looks and feels better when the momentum comes from the grass roots. It is important to find the natural group to organize and to look for strengths within the group.

Many of the Reading Recovery teachers were facing the loss of jobs or seeing coworkers lose theirs. But most important, we all recognized that losing the Reading Recovery program would mean the loss of an entire community of readers. Reading Recovery teachers are experts in childhood literacy and are passionate about what they do. Although we were fighting a difficult battle, we started out on a positive basis by relying on the strengths and savvy of our group members.

Finding a balance when organizing so that you meet often enough to keep the lines of communication open, but not so often as to make meetings unproductive, can be tricky. It can also be difficult to create a sense of cohesiveness in a school district with thirty elementary schools, nine middle schools, and five high schools, as in the Madison district, or in rural communities where less populated districts cover a large area. For this reason, it is important to organize a small group of people to lay the foundation for the work of the larger group.

Call a meeting only if you have something to say. If you have meetings simply to have meetings, you'll start losing supporters. Have a written agenda for each meeting so that people can see that you have thought about the meeting ahead of time and that there are specific points to cover. (See Appendix B: Small Group Meeting Agendas.) In our case, the agenda had a single focus— to organize supporters to appear at board of education meetings.

To accomplish the established goal, provide as many ways as possible for people to be involved and to leave the meeting knowing they have something to do. They can talk with supporters who were not able to attend the meeting and update them. They can call or write or meet with officials. They can be responsible for bringing food to the next meeting. (See Appendix C: Twenty-Five Ways You Can Be Involved.)

In 1964, the year after the Birmingham, Alabama, lunch counter sit-ins and demonstrations, Martin Luther King Jr. published *Why We Can't Wait.*

He includes in it a copy of the Commitment Card that all nonviolent demonstrators were required to sign. It is a dramatic pledge of personal and moral commitment in which signers make a number of pledges—to sacrifice so that all may be free, to be of service to others, and to refrain from violence of fist, tongue, or heart. At the bottom of the card, below the signature, is the following paragraph:

> Besides demonstrations, I could also help the movement by: (Circle the proper items) Run errands, Drive my car, Fix food for volunteers, Clerical work, Make phone calls, Answer phones, Mimeograph, Type, Print signs, Distribute leaflets. (King 1964, 64)

King built a movement with passion and zeal. He also achieved his goals by recognizing how important it is to organize the situation so that many different people feel they can contribute something. Those who weren't suited for nonviolent protest were still asked to run errands, make phone calls, type letters. That is how things get done—with lots of people contributing, in lots of ways.

To help keep your group going and to stay together, take two or three minutes at each meeting to talk about the progress you are making. Report the current number of supporters (see Appendix D). Discuss why it is so important to keep working on one issue. Personalize your cause if you can. Refer to one specific child whose life will be changed because of what you are doing. Tell a story about how another volunteer became inspired. You don't need to be a great public speaker. Just speak from the heart.

Meetings are not the only way to keep people together. Communicating effectively is essential to the success of any campaign. Be especially aware of how your group of supporters finds it easiest to communicate. Some people love e-mail. Others prefer to use the phone, while still others don't like to use the phone at all. In our campaign, other Reading Recovery teachers found their niche in communicating by writing letters. (See Appendixes E, F, G, and H.) Be creative in getting the word out.

To keep costs low, whenever possible use workplace mailboxes or fax machines, or simply post a notice on restroom or lounge doors. Whenever and however you can get your message out to the larger group, even if it means passing notes, do it. We suggest you use what is easiest and most effective. If you are concerned about disciplinary actions resulting from your activities, check your district's written policies or your teacher contract.

In Regie Routman's *Literacy at the Crossroads: Becoming Political in Our Schools* Chapter 4 is entitled "The Need to Be Articulate, Astute, and Active."

The title for our work could be "The Need Is to Talk, Talk, Talk, Listen, Listen, Listen, and Work, Work, Work." That's how you organize.

Organize Around One Focus: Board of Education Meetings

Attending board of education meetings was the most important thing we did. The meetings provided a public forum to get our message heard. Although school districts in regions of the country operate differently, the best forum we all have to use is our public school board meetings. These gatherings provide opportunities to inform the general public about issues and to make your case to members of the school board, who will ultimately decide if the program will continue.

This section describes how we organized for board of education meetings. However, the broad brush of what we are saying can be applied to organizing any focused action: plan the large scale of your action; pay attention to details; stand up politically for what you believe.

Our presence was strong at board meetings because we made sure we had speakers from all sectors of our community. As Reading Recovery teachers we have taught the children of political leaders, university professors, refugees, church administrators, poor families, and middle class families. At our first board meeting, to make sure we would be noticed, we had twelve speakers representing people from every part of our district. At subsequent meetings we scaled back to three to five speakers so as not to monopolize the board meetings.

Orchestrating a school board presentation requires deciding who should speak and in what order they should appear. It is important not to appear self-serving, so it is better to let others do the talking for you. For our first few appearances we opened with a teacher who had a working knowledge of our program, followed by parents across the economic spectrum. (See Appendix I for an example of a prepared speech.) Who speaks is important, and a diverse group makes for an effective presentation. Our speakers included former Reading Recovery teachers, classroom teachers, many parents, students, influential community figures, and business leaders. Someone from our group concluded our appearance. We brainstormed answers to possible questions ahead of time. No matter what the question, we tried to give one of our prepared answers to get our point across.

Understanding the organization of school board meetings is crucial. Pay close attention to detail and find out how your system works. In our district, a form must be filled out if you wish to speak. (The Public Appearance Registration Form is provided in appendix J.) A completed form is also required if you wish to register in support of a particular issue, but do not wish to speak. If you have a similar system, make sure that you have the proper form filled out correctly. One strategy is to bombard the board with as many forms as possible registering support of your issue. Then the total number of supporters will be officially noted.

Have a plan of action for your speakers. To ensure an organized presentation, submit forms in the order that you wish speakers to testify. Make sure all speakers are at the front of the room and ready, so as not to annoy the board with dead time as you search for the next speaker.

Vary your speakers and keep them steadily flowing to the podium, indicating a fluid stream of concern for your issue. Don't try to overwhelm the board. Ten speakers in a row giving two- to three-minute talks with no repetition is effective. Twenty people spread out over the course of an evening all saying the same thing is less effective.

Be as considerate as possible to those you have asked to speak. Provide transportation to the meeting if necessary. If speakers are unsure of what to say, offer to help them organize their talks. We heard parents who spoke from their hearts and from their own experiences. Even when it meant speaking through an interpreter, parents needed little encouragement to stand up to tell of the important role that Reading Recovery had played in their children's lives.

Some parents were so proud of how well their children now read that they brought them along to read to the board. A few children even came forward on their own and wanted to speak for us. Having children speak worked well in Madison and visibly touched some board members. In other places, having children as your representatives might not work as well. Be aware of your community, and plan accordingly.

You will have a stronger presence if, in addition to speakers, you have a short, concise handout that makes your point in another way. At the first school board meeting we attended, Reading Recovery teachers were handing out a sheet with statistics showing how well our former students did on the Wisconsin Third Grade Reading Test. On the back of this sheet, we had comments from parents, teachers, and administrators in support of Reading Recovery. We had culled these responses from Reading Recovery Annual Reports to the board. (See Appendixes K and L.) You might also want to give selected articles to school board members *after* completing your presentations, so that school board members are not distracted by reading the articles while you are speaking.

You do not have to do everything yourself in organizing public appearances. Prepare a list of tasks for the agenda of your group meetings, and let people choose items for which they will be responsible. Offer something for everyone. Find members who can arrive early to distribute the handouts at the door. Make sure the teacher who contacted parents or other speakers is there to greet them, so speakers feel more at ease and know what they need to do. You might have members of the audience hold signs supporting your cause. Arrange for someone to be responsible for taking notes, especially recording any questions or comments from board members. Have another person assigned to simply watch the body language of administrators and members of the board. Knowing what speakers they responded to will help you to plan both future appearances and individual meetings with board members.

Make every attempt to get speakers on the agenda as early in the meeting as possible. We arranged this by going early to each board meeting with the forms filled out and in the order we wanted speakers to appear. Then one of us was sure to be first in line to hand the forms to the public information officer. In this way our speakers were always among the first at the meetings. (See Appendix M: Instructions for Participation at School Board Meetings.)

Arriving early, besides being a courtesy to your speakers, also provides an opportunity to get to know the person who is responsible for letting you in the door. The public information officer can be another useful ally. He or she knows better than anyone how the board meetings operate and may be able to give you helpful tips on how to organize your appearances most effectively.

In Madison, some school board meetings were budget hearings open to the public. Others were committee meetings at which we could be present, but not speak. We got a calendar of all the various meetings from the board secretary and we made sure each meeting was covered. Even when we had no opportunity to speak, we still sent one or two people to the smaller meetings. Regular attendance keeps the board aware of your issue and improves your visibility. If they keep seeing you, they can't forget you and they know that the issue you represent will not go away.

Whether we like it or not, many times we go into the political arena as adversaries of our employers. We need to do our best to eliminate barriers between us, while using the democratic system to serve our best interests. If in the process of making your case heard, a few feathers get ruffled, at least you know someone heard you.

After our first presentation, we learned through the grapevine that the administration would prefer that we not continue appearing. Some members of our group immediately thought it was best to stop going. We then spent crucial time encouraging our own members not to cave in to the wishes of the administration. School board meetings are opportunities to inform the general public about an issue, and to make a case to members of the school board who will ultimately decide if your program will continue. By appearing at the board, you are exercising your democratic right. If we had stopped organizing board appearances, our program would have been cut. It's that simple. When things get a little frightening, you don't need to start out with a lot of courage to stand up for what you believe in. Standing up for what you believe in will *give* you courage. We learned that.

Work with Your Union

We are fortunate to belong to one of the strongest teachers' unions in the state, Madison Teachers, Inc. (MTI). Comprised of 2,600 members, MTI is the second largest teachers' union in Wisconsin. As members of MTI, we were able to draw upon political expertise, contacts, and clout. In other areas where teachers' unions are not as strong, parent coalitions may provide the same kinds of expertise and contacts that we built through our union.

Do not underestimate the political expertise that your teachers' union can provide. We had meetings with our executive director, John Matthews, to discuss our strategy and to get his advice. After years of representing us at the bargaining table, John has gained a well-deserved reputation as a shrewd advocate for teachers' rights. When we would forget to broaden our public visibility, he would put us back on course. He suggested holding a press conference to make the public aware of the Reading Recovery program cuts, and when we did not follow up on it, he suggested it again. The second time we listened.

We held our press conference at union headquarters, and John made phone calls for us to each of the newspapers and to the television and radio stations. With John calling, they knew it was an event not to miss.

John was a sounding board, too. At that crucial point after our first board appearance when we got the indirect message to stop coming, John told us that our instinct was right and that we had to keep appearing; we had to maintain a public presence.

The proposed cuts in Reading Recovery were announced to us during a pivotal school board election. Two school board members were up for reelection, and the endorsement of MTI Voters, the political action arm of the union, is always coveted and critical. (See Appendix N: MTI Voters School Board Election Questionnaire.) One incumbent was not sympathetic to teachers, and we, as Reading Recovery teachers, sensed that he would also not support the Reading Recovery program. When MTI Voters endorsed the candidate opposing the incumbent school board member, Reading Recovery teachers came out in force to support the union-endorsed candidate. Working with other unions and community members, we ousted the unsympathetic incumbent and helped to replace him with someone with whom Reading Recovery teachers had already established a good working relationship.

The influence of the teachers' union may not be felt as strongly in other areas as MTI is in our district. Every executive director and political action group may not be as powerful as ours. But the structure and organization of a union will still be available as a source to help you. Just as we needed to find out about the structure of the school board meetings, we needed to become familiar with the workings of the union. For instance, we have monthly faculty representative council meetings. We started attending the faculty representative meetings and brought the proposed cuts in Reading Recovery to the attention of union leadership.

Do not assume that union leadership will necessarily know about your issue. Our leaders, deeply committed to teachers, were not initially aware of the proposed cuts in Reading Recovery. Once they were informed, they tried to figure out how they could support us, and they made our issue a priority. Work with your union by keeping them informed, and by volunteering to work on your issue within the union structure.

Madison Teachers, Inc., has a great deal of clout in the city of Madison and in the rest of Wisconsin. When teachers decided that an issue such as Reading Recovery was important, even teachers who were not directly affected volunteered to help. "Our union makes us strong" is the motto of MTI. The same applies to us as teachers in the United States. Teaching makes us strong. Teachers, strongly unionized, with combined political action, have the potential to make a difference.

John Matthews, the executive director of MTI, once said, "Some people dream of success, while others wake up and work hard at it. If we are among the latter, success will be ours. Overcoming the seemingly impossible only takes a little more creativity than overcoming the very difficult." John also recommended that we read Saul Alinsky's *Rules for Radicals* and *Reveille for Radicals*. The following statement from *Reveille for Radicals* illustrates the political importance of organizing:

Let all apostles of planning never forget that what is most important in life is substance rather than structure. The substance of a democracy is its people and if that substance is good—if the people are healthy, interested, informed, participating, filled with faith in themselves and others—then the structure will inevitably reflect its substance. (56)

Establish and Maintain Connections with the Media

By making such a strong presentation at that first board meeting, we gained the attention of both morning and afternoon newspapers. The reporter from the morning paper came to Barb to ask questions; the afternoon reporter approached Susan. We responded to their interest by being accessible, providing information, discussing the issue with them, and continuing our public presence so that our issue remained news.

It can be intimidating to talk with reporters. You don't know what they will ask, or what they will report. But you need them to get your issue to the public. And they need you because they need news.

In preparation for our press conference we met with a parent supporter who had a public relations background. Because she had witnessed Reading Recovery's effect on her son, she willingly helped us by writing a press release. She also fashioned a sound-bite script for Barb to deliver in front of television cameras. (These transcripts can be found in the Appendixes O and P.)

The more you talk with reporters, the easier it becomes. Invite them, as we did, to come and see the importance of your work in the schools. Just as we would do with board members (see page 25), we invited the reporters to observe Reading Recovery lessons and discuss them afterwards. It is easier to talk over a longer period of time with a reporter—you feel less pressure to get your point exactly right because you know you can come back to it and clarify it if necessary—than it is to answer quick questions in a hall after a meeting.

We also found that the reporters enjoyed having someone to talk with in more depth about the issues. Their job is thinking about education (or, if there is not a specific education reporter, about the city or town), but they rarely get a chance to discuss their own perspective. If you spend a sustained period of time with a reporter, you can go into greater depth and have more say in framing the discussion. The *Capital Times* reporter stayed long into Susan's planning time after observing her teach, because Susan had asked him what *he* thought. The interview became a discussion, and the reporter started asking more abstract, open-ended questions about education that reflected how much he had been thinking about the issues beyond what he was able to write. He gained real background information on the situation that would influence how he wrote about the issue. Susan gained respect for how much work he put into his job, and a professional relationship was established. He took Susan's phone calls, and Susan took his. After that long discussion, it was much easier to answer the reporter's questions than it would have been in the rush of that first board meeting.

Put another way, if you find yourself in a difficult situation with someone, try to imagine what it is like to be that person rather than yourself. Reporters have a job to produce news stories every day. If you help them by giving them interesting news and respecting their job, they will probably report you positively. Don't expect to get everything you want, just the way you want it, in the paper or on TV or radio. But if you respect reporters, and speak honestly about your issue, they will probably be fair to you. Establish and maintain a relationship with the press by helping them to do their job (see Appendix Q).

Your movement needs to be visible and vocal on a larger level, too. Every letter to the editor doesn't get printed, but the *number* of letters on an issue, or the number of phone calls to a radio show or afternoon local news show, influences how or whether a story is covered. Assign writing or calling the different newspapers and television and radio stations as specific jobs people can do.

Establish and Maintain
Connections with the Board

Behind-the-scenes work is crucial to your cause. Board members may be impressed by your supporters at meetings and still remain opposed to your issue. Meet with board members one-on-one to find out where they stand, to answer questions they may have, and to start lining up their support. You need a majority of the board to vote in your favor (see Appendix R).

At our meetings with Reading Recovery teachers, we assigned one teacher to each board member, then discussed how best to talk to each individual. Each Reading Recovery teacher invited her assigned board member to see a lesson in her school and scheduled the lesson so that there would be time afterward to talk, either over lunch or a free period. The opportunity to see the teacher at work and relate to her as a person cemented a positive relationship.

To lobby effectively, it is important to find out what makes each board member tick. Learn what a board member's issues are, and speak about your concern in those terms. Aware that one board member was annoyed that statistics repeatedly showed black children in a poor light, we used statistics that demonstrated the success of minority children in the Reading Recovery program. We were also careful to point out that economic factors, not race, were much better indicators of the probable success of a child in the program. The data won over that particular member, and we were able to secure his vote.

If money is the issue, and it usually is, talk about the cost-effectiveness of your program. We explained to board members that Reading Recovery serves approximately three hundred children from the bottom of their classes each year, at half-time wages. The overwhelming majority of those children learn to read, needing no further extra help in school. That's cost-effective!

Never assume that decision makers will know the intricacies or even the generalities of your program. They have too many other programs to understand, and you need to let them know what is essential about yours. (See Appendixes S and T for other sources we used.) To get to the core, we referred over and over to the data from the Wisconsin Third Grade Reading Test because they showed that our Reading Recovery students continue as successful readers.

One of our most conservative board members said in conversation with us, "Anyone can have a child who can't read." He is right. We quoted that remark often to persuade other board members to think along the same lines and to connect differing views with common concerns.

As we continued to talk with board members, we started counting votes. We knew we had three. We needed four. We focused on the two board members who were wavering; we kept listening to them to find out what they needed to hear to vote for our program. At the same time, we worked with another board member on creating the necessary language for a budget amendment to reinstate Reading Recovery positions. You may need someone to propose amendments for you and be aware that amendments will have to be turned in by a certain date.

The unexpected happened. The superintendent's own final budget proposal restored all of the cut Reading Recovery positions. We had focused primarily on the board, because we had the most public access to them as elected officials. But by repeatedly appearing at the board meetings, we had convinced the superintendent of the value of our program. We thought back then to the interest she had shown in the parents when they spoke, how often she leaned forward when parents were really speaking from their heart. As an astute administrator, the sheer number of parents who supported us did not escape her attention. But probably what most helped her to change her mind was how closely Reading Recovery's results mesh with her goal that every child know how to read by the end of third grade. Again, do not assume that even those in charge of your program will know its power. They have many other responsibilities. It is your job to let them know why your program is necessary.

What to Do After You Win or Lose

Your issue isn't over when the vote is taken because, next year, the vote will come up again. It seems that in Wisconsin, as in much of the rest of the country, the next budget will be even tighter.

If you lose, resolve to come back again. If you win, celebrate, and then resolve to come back again.

Work on school board, local, state, and national campaigns. At a local level, you will get to know the school board members and will be able to talk with much more ease than when you made your first appointment to meet with them. Having gained respect for your knowledge and commitment, they will see you as a source to turn to for information on the schools, and they will see your endorsement as a necessary one to gain for the next school board race.

If you disagree with how a member votes, the next election is an opportunity to try to replace that member. Stay involved. You will make a difference.

Volunteer to serve on state and local educational association committees. You will make important contacts and gain a better understanding of how decisions are made.

Continue to attend committee and budget hearings. The more you know about how your school district works, the more effective your strategy decisions will be.

By calling that first meeting when we didn't know yet what we should do, we took the first step in changing the school board budget. That first step led us down a long road, and we learned a great deal along the way.

Because of the state-imposed revenue caps, money for education is hard to find in our state now. But because we kept our message simple and would not go away, the board and superintendent listened to us. Reading Recovery became part of the superintendent's gateway plan in reading, which has as its goal all children becoming readers by the end of third grade. Children are learning to read in Madison because of what we did. As Martin Luther King Jr. said, "The time is always right to do what is right."

And now is the right time to be politically active.

3

How to Think
and Act Politically

IT IS NOT ONLY ORGANIZING, BUT ORGANIZING EFFECTIVELY
that matters in political action. Thinking politically helps you to keep your
"eyes on the prize," to maintain your focus as you organize. It helps you to
remember to build relationships as you work; it saves you time because you
are more effective in what you do.

In this chapter we elaborate on aspects of thinking politically—learning from other political leaders, creating a focus, and knowing who makes
decisions. We discuss important parts of acting politically—providing leadership; speaking publicly and talking with the press; being organized. We end
with final thoughts on political action for education—doing it because it's
the right thing to do and an important part of political action that is rarely
addressed, taking care of yourself as you organize.

Learn from Those Who
Have Come Before You

As a grassroots organizer, you are probably beginning with little power or
money to advance your cause. The nonviolent movements led by Mahatma
Gandhi and Martin Luther King Jr. began in just this way, as small, specific,
local actions; they are models for how to organize your movement.

Leaders of nonviolence and democratic movements often faced dangers of imprisonment and death for their stands. Though in organizing for
education in the United States, we do not face the dangers that King and

29

Gandhi faced, our actions can follow the same principles as nonviolent movements. We are doing this to make children's lives better. We are often doing this to stand up for people who can't speak for themselves. As Coretta Scott King describes it in *The Words of Martin Luther King, Jr.*, King didn't set out to lead a civil rights movement, or even to lead a year-long boycott of the buses in Montgomery, Alabama. He had planned to be a Baptist preacher in a large Southern congregation. But when Rosa Parks was arrested for refusing to give up her seat on the bus, he offered his church as a meeting place to discuss the idea of a black boycott of the buses, and then was elected by his peers to lead the boycott. He became a national civil rights leader by being drawn by his convictions into involvement in a single, local issue. (Don't worry—we're not asking you to become national leaders. We're trying to show the power of focused, local involvement.)

Mahatma Gandhi created and led a strong Indian presence in South Africa and then led the struggle for India's independence from British rule, in large part through a series of focused, local actions. He led indigo growers in Bihar in protesting the profits they were required to give to landlords. He then helped textile workers in Ahmadabad. Each time he worked locally on one issue. Even after he had become a national leader, he continued to lead his nonviolent movement through a series of single, focused actions: the spinning of cloth as a symbol of Indian self-sufficiency and reminder of the vast number of Indians who lived in poverty, the Salt March in protest of British taxation and rule, his famous fasts as a reaction to specific injustices.

There are other leaders of nonviolent political practice whose actions and words are just as inspiring. Thich Nhat Hanh, a leader of the peace movement in Vietnam, wrote to his followers from exile in France when several in Vietnam had been kidnapped and murdered, and others faced real danger. This letter, later published as *The Miracle of Mindfulness*, reminded followers to remain aware of the present moment and of their presence in it, to continue to see the beauty in life in the face of hatred and danger.

Saul Alinsky became an American folk hero for his leadership in organizing at a grassroots level. He distrusted money and power, and believed firmly in democracy. Nothing was sacred to Alinsky, except, perhaps, the force of people coming together for a common community cause.

Václav Havel, the president of the Czech Republic, was, under Soviet rule, a noted dissident, writer, and member of the Czech human rights movement who was imprisoned for his actions. He writes stirringly about democracy and sees politics as "morality in practice." For example, he rejects the so-called reasonable solution of apathy or defeatism:

Throughout my life, whenever I have thought aloud about public affairs, about civic, political, and moral matters, some reasonable person has inevitably pointed out, in the name of reason, that I, too, should be reasonable, should put aside my wild ideas, and accept once and for all that nothing can change for the better because the world is divided forever into two parts. Both these half-worlds are content with this division, and neither wants to change. It is pointless to behave according to one's conscience, because no one can change anything. . . .

I was far from the only one to disregard such wisdom. There were many of us in my country who continued to do what we thought right. We were not afraid of being considered fools. We went on thinking about how to make the world a better place, and we made no secret of our ideas. (Havel 1997, 32–33)

We want to highlight two qualities in particular of these leaders. First, they read and learned from other writers. Gandhi read Henry David Thoreau while in prison in South Africa. King read Gandhi in seminary and credits Gandhi's emphasis on love and nonviolence as the basis of King's own method of social reform. King and Thich Nhat Hanh met during the Vietnam War, and King was so moved by Nhat Hanh that he subsequently nominated him for the Nobel Peace Prize. Havel read Jefferson and other writers on democracy while living in a totalitarian state. They helped him to dream.

If, with the added responsibility of acting politically now, you feel you have no time for books, then read a page as you fall asleep at night; carry a copy of one of these inspirational books to pull out when you're waiting for a meeting to begin, or to read along with your students during Sustained Silent Reading. The bibliography contains suggested readings by these and other authors.

Second, and just as important, each leader saw the world with a hope that was grounded in their actions in the present (what King referred to as "the fierce urgency of *now*"). They also despaired, but they repeatedly returned to hope. Gandhi disbanded his satyagraha movement in 1922 when a gathering in support of his movement turned violent; in 1926 he withdrew for a year from national politics. King wrote from jail in Birmingham of his disappointment in white churches that they weren't supporting the civil rights movement. Nhat Hanh went into a five-year period of retreat after unsuccessful attempts to rescue boat people escaping from Vietnam. But each came back from despair to act publicly and socially for good and for peace.

There is a broad range of styles in nonviolent leaders. Gandhi's practice grew from (and at the same time nurtured) a strict morality that sees us each as responsible for ourselves, for all beings, and for Truth. (The name of his nonviolent movement, *satyagraha*, can be translated into English as "truth force.") King, with keen intellectual understanding, raged against long-standing injustice with the measured response of nonviolence. There was an intense equanimity to King, an urgent calm that underlay his actions. His hope and belief were in the future and in his God. His hope also drew strength from the power of a large movement growing, bringing together people from all walks of life. Alinsky, on the other hand, was irreverent and distrusted power. He drew his energy from disrupting the status quo and seeing community build. Nhat Hanh's practice, finally, is grounded in the fullness of the present moment. He emphasizes the interconnection of all in the world and teaches developing awareness of compassion and of our place among others. One of these leaders will probably appeal more to you than the others. That's the one to read.

In standing up for public education, in organizing at a grassroots level, you are defending a cornerstone of democracy. Thomas Jefferson repeatedly wrote about the importance of an educated populace to democracy. He closely linked citizenry and access to public education:[1]

> I know of no safe depositary of the ultimate powers of the society but the people themselves; and if we think them not enlightened enough to exercise their control with a wholesome discretion, the remedy is not to take it from them, but to inform their discretion by education. This is the true corrective of abuses of constitutional power. (To William C. Jarvis, 1820)

> Every government degenerates when trusted to the rulers of the people alone. The people themselves, therefore, are its only safe depositories. And to render even them safe, their minds must be improved to a certain degree. (Notes on Virginia, 1782)

> Convinced that the people are the only safe depositories of their own liberty, and that they are not safe unless enlightened to a certain degree, I have looked on our present state of liberty as a short-lived possession unless the mass of the people could be informed to a certain degree. (To Littleton Waller Tazewell, 1805)

> The information of the people at large can alone make them the safe as

---

1. All of these quotations are taken from a web site created by Eyler Robert Coates Sr. and devoted to the writings of Jefferson: http://etext.virginia.edu/jefferson/quotations/jeff1350.html. Coates has taken quotations from Jefferson's writings on politics and government and organized them into thirty-five different topics. Readers are encouraged to quote freely from them.

they are the sole depositary of our political and religious freedom. (To William Duane, 1810)

Quote Jefferson to help yourself and others to begin to speak again of democracy as necessarily secured by a well-educated people.

Find Your Main Focus and Organize Around That

Have one focus and make sure everyone involved in your movement knows what it is. For us, it was getting parents and teachers to speak at every public board meeting from the time the program cuts were announced until the final vote was taken on the budget. This meant we had speakers at meetings over a period of several months, and we had to keep ourselves and teachers involved for those months. If teachers in your district cannot speak at school board meetings, your focus could be finding parents to represent you. Or your focus might be meetings with administrators or elected officials. In any case, remember that if you keep your issue a public one, it will generate more interest and power for your position.

Martin Luther King Jr. came to the same conclusion about the importance of one focus, as the following self-evaluation reveals:

> In analyzing our campaign in Albany, Georgia, we decided that one of the principal mistakes we had made there was to scatter our efforts too widely. We had been so involved in attacking segregation in general that we had failed to direct our protest effectively to any one major facet. We concluded that . . . a more effective battle could be waged if it was concentrated against one aspect of the evil and intricate system of segregation. (King 1964, 54)

Give good thought to what you think will be the one activity that is most effective and will bring people together with a common purpose. With a clear focus, you can see clear results, and that will help to keep people involved. One of the most important results we saw was the excitement created by the appearances at that first board meeting.

At our first school board meeting, we had twelve speakers. We had no trouble finding parents to speak for us because of the roughly fifty Reading Recovery teachers in the Madison area, we had a group of about fifteen who regularly attended our larger organizing meetings. (Most meetings had around twenty-five people at them, with different teachers coming to some, but not all, meetings. In total, probably forty-five of the fifty Reading Recovery teachers were involved in some way over those several months.)

Those fifty teachers had touched hundreds of children's lives in their Reading Recovery teaching. Not every parent will be aware of how profoundly teachers have changed their children's lives or be willing to speak in front of the school board. But a real advantage in organizing teachers is that good teachers will have parents who realize what they have done for their children and appreciate it. From that core group of fifteen teachers, we came up with around twenty-five parents who spoke for us over three months. That meant that each of us had to recruit only one or two parents, and that was not hard to do.

It is unusual for twelve speakers to appear at a board meeting to speak to one issue, but it is even more unusual for them to come from all over the city, from different social classes and ethnic groups. The spectrum of our speakers caught the board's attention: a father who was an internationally known professor of communications at the University of Wisconsin–Madison; two Hmong refugee mothers who addressed the board through an interpreter; a welfare mother who saw Reading Recovery change the life not only of her child who was in the program, but of her next child who learned to read because of the example of his brother; a mother from one of the best-known families in town; a former school board member, an accomplished, confident speaker who broke down in tears describing the change Reading Recovery had made in her son's life.

The power of the parents' words brought a stillness to the room. You could feel the interest and attention grow as parent after parent spoke from their hearts. Upper middle-class parents told of how their houses were full of books, they had read to their children from birth, but their children had been at the bottom of their classes, and hadn't learned to read until Reading Recovery. When Bob McChesney, the University of Wisconsin communications professor, started to speak, the *Capital Times* reporter, who knew McChesney's intellectual work, moved to the front of the room and started taking notes.

When the Hmong mothers, Xay Xiong and Pa Yang, spoke through interpreters, the president of the school board and several other members leaned forward, intent on listening. When the former school board member spoke, and her voice suddenly dropped registers as she fought back tears, her friends on the board were with her, and knew the depths from which her words came. Parents and teachers in the audience were wiping their eyes as she continued to speak.

Right at that moment, in that meeting, our movement solidified.

As luck would have it, a fifth-grade boy, Lázaro Medina, who was at the school board meeting with his mother to see a new board member sworn in, had been a Reading Recovery student in first grade. He hadn't known Reading Recovery would be a topic that night, but as he listened to speakers, he told his mother that he, too, wanted to speak about Reading Recovery. Unbeknownst to us, right there in the auditorium, he composed a speech and came forward to tell his story of how Reading Recovery had changed his life.

Teachers in the auditorium were inspired by the parents' and Lázaro's words. The feeling was so strong that after the meeting, we spoke to each other with few words, communicating instead simply by looking at each other and nodding or holding each other tight. The teachers carried that feeling with them back to their buildings, and the number of teachers supporting us and willing to get involved grew.

Because our first appearance before the board was so well focused, our campaign had become a public issue. Making sure people continued coming to the board kept Reading Recovery a public issue. Throughout those months, our focus continued to be lining up speakers for the next meeting. Once that goal was accomplished, we undertook plenty of other actions. But speakers at the board always came first.

Once you have your focus and the group is going forward with it, don't squelch other people's creativity or elaboration. Kathy Levin and Joyce Dewey organized a letter campaign from parents all over the city. Lisa Glueck and Sara Clark carefully crafted a letter, addressed to the board and superintendent from all Reading Recovery teachers, that ended up in the morning paper as a featured guest column. Jane Ross wrote a Reading Recovery rap that she taught to both her first-grade students and former students ranging into fifth grade. She brought them to the board to perform the rap. As long as you are keeping to your focus, encourage other people's ideas.

Provide Leadership and Direction

The movement leader's two most important contributions are to establish the group's focus and to build a movement. You build a movement by recognizing what people do and by encouraging them in the ways they are involved. When people have ideas that are different from yours, these two actions may at times seem in conflict with each other. Here are some thoughts on ways to pull them together.

First, give serious consideration to what you think is the best focus before you meet with a large group of people. As a leader, it is crucial to focus the principal energy of the movement. If you can, before you bring a larger group of people together, think out with one, or at most two, other people what will be your main objective. Then, have ready at your first large-group meeting a clear written agenda with that focus the main point on it. This will allow you to spend your time at the meeting talking about *how* to accomplish your goal, rather than *what* to accomplish.

More than likely, having thought out what action to take beforehand and having an agenda to follow will keep the meeting focused on that action. If at that first large meeting, however, people object to the focus you present and have six different ideas about what to do, then it is time to listen as carefully as you can to them. Thich Nhat Hanh calls this "deep listening." Listen to individuals and to the sense of the whole meeting, and be willing to see the value in what people want to do. Present your own points clearly. As the person who had the interest and impetus to call the meeting, you may have spent more time thinking about the issue than others. Make it clear that taking a public action will attract interest from the media. See if there is some way to synthesize what others want to do with what you think should be the principal action. Listening carefully to others and valuing their ideas will help you to build a movement. Being an autocrat will not. (Volunteer movements don't last terribly long with autocratic leaders.)

Even once your focus is established, it can be difficult to maintain it. In the first few weeks of organizing to save the Reading Recovery program, after the large meeting at Susan's house, we had several meetings with five or so core people to continue to plan and organize. Somehow, these meetings turned into further discussions of what we should do now. There were many different ideas about how best to proceed—letter-writing campaigns to parents and board members, gathering data, appearing at the board. The meetings didn't have clear results and led to other meetings that also didn't resolve into clear political action. The energy of the most committed people was becoming sidetracked, rather than being focused productively to advocate for our program. King called this tendency amidst the excitement of political organizing *the paralysis of analysis.*

This was a difficult time in our campaign, and the one we learned the most from. In the first large group, we had already established as our focus appearances before the board, and teachers had agreed on it. But now, working with our most committed members, we weren't moving forward, and differences of opinion were starting to cause divisions among us. We had to learn about maintaining a very difficult balance in political organizing: keep moving forward with your focus, and . . . don't be too attached to one unchanging concept of what that focus is.

The trick is to know your focus, and yet at the same time stay open to others' ideas, incorporating them if possible. For example, at first the letter-writing campaign seemed to us to conflict with our focus on appearances before the board. However, when viewed from a different perspective, apparently disparate actions may become a part of your focus. In June the collected letters were presented to the board, and the stack of letters made a very strong statement. As long as you have enough people to get your central action accomplished, be willing to broaden your definition of that action. Don't keep meeting and talking and discussing; find ways instead for your group to go out and *do*.

There is a necessary flip side to being flexible enough about your focus to include as many actions and volunteers as possible. A volunteer movement needs leadership that will shift wide-ranging discussions into commitment to a clear course of action. This is a crucial point, not to spend forever debating as a group what you will do. And it is showing real respect for the volunteers you are working with, because it is valuing their time.

Regie Routman makes a similar point about providing structure in *Literacy at the Crossroads*, when she asks if sometimes it is possible to be too democratic. There are points in *structuring* a political movement when trying to listen to everyone will take the energy away from your cause. This doesn't mean, of course, that you should not listen to people. It means instead to give them a clear framework to work in.

In our specific situation, meetings with a core group of five leaders moved us away from action. If you are working at a statewide level or in a larger group, working with such a core group may be exactly what is needed. However, if your movement does not have a primary focus and is turning into a series of meetings and not actions, you will need to provide leadership. Help your group find a focus that will enable you all to act.

In our campaign, Barb and Susan found it a boon to have each other to work with in leading the movement. If you can find a person with whom you work well, he or she will be there to bounce ideas off, check out strategy with, keep you on the path, share responsibility, and pull you up when you're down.

We worked well together, because we recognized we have different skills and that we benefit from bringing those skills together. We are both organized, but in very different ways. Barb has a quick mind that cuts to the core of a matter. She is adept at following through on making sure that what has been planned gets done. Barb can also be light and can schmooze with people, an important skill in smoothing out difficult situations. She pays attention to details and deadlines.

Susan led by having her heart in what she did. She is organized at the level of keeping things moving forward, of keeping the momentum and interest of the group. She gets her point across clearly, but she also listens carefully to others, and sees their strengths. She has the patience for the big picture.

If you are leading a movement, consider what your skills are and how they mesh with those of your colleagues. Then capitalize on your strengths.

We often had different viewpoints on strategy or what to do next, but we knew how to consider the other's viewpoint and often came up with a third perspective that was better than either of the two points we had started with. Work on developing that kind of relationship, too, if you share leadership with another person.

We were lucky enough to work well together, but we realize that that doesn't always happen. You may need to lead alone. In this case, you will especially appreciate the other volunteers.

Volunteers in grassroots efforts usually have full lives. Many have families, children, parents, jobs, and other commitments. The time you and the other volunteers can give to your cause is bound to be limited. In your role as a leader of a volunteer grassroots movement, make sure people can see clear results from what they do. Your leadership lies in helping people to find what they can do best and always letting them know you are aware they have done it. This reinforcement is vital to keep people coming back.

Volunteer political action at a grassroots level comes from a passion or belief in the importance of what is being done. It comes from a sense of connection to the world and responsibility in it. Unfortunately, apathy and skepticism are more common reactions to politics in our age. Value the beliefs that motivate those who come to act with you. Admire this commitment in others and thank them for it. In the process, you will come to feel more a part of a movement, one citizen connected with another.

The relationships you form with other people will be part of what energizes you and keeps you going in your volunteer work. Take the time to recognize the importance of those relationships and to appreciate what you are building.

Build a Coalition

Without the hard work of all the other teachers and parents, we could not have saved our program. Recognize that as a leader, that is all you are. You are a leader, not a movement. And without a movement, your leadership wouldn't be terribly effective.

Be aware of the importance of what other people are doing, and thank them for it. This doesn't mean that what you are doing *isn't* important—a movement needs a leader—but to build a coalition you must value other people and let them know that. If you are part of a group of teachers, reach out to parents. If you are parents, reach out to teachers.

Sometimes it can be discouraging if other people do not show the same commitment that you do. However, a movement is made up of a range of people. Some people thrive on political action. Other people have never been involved before and may be hesitant and even afraid. It is important to recognize each participant's strength.

As mentioned in Chapter 2, Appendix C lists twenty-five ways to be involved in political action. All these aspects of being involved—driving parents to the board meeting, arranging a phone tree, coming to meetings, providing food—are important. You build a movement by getting people involved, and people can start out (or remain) involved in small and large ways. You will see both happen. Value not only the large but also the small contribution. It means one more person is a part of and cares about your campaign. Whatever people do, it will make them feel involved, will build your movement, and will get needed things done. Thank people for what they do, including board members who take the time to come to your class, talk to you on the phone, or meet you for coffee. Building a movement is building relationships and respecting other people.

Appreciating whatever it is people do, in itself, broadens your base of support. Maintaining a positive attitude also helps you to focus on the main tasks, instead of feeling frustrated that others are not as involved as you. Everyone will not be intently involved. Still, the more people you get involved in a small way, the stronger your movement will be.

Recognize, too, that you are not always the best person to do something. Some teachers thought that Barb and Susan were doing the wrong thing by organizing so strongly to save Reading Recovery. They thought that we should just accept the budget decisions that had been made. If we had tried to encourage them to become involved, we would have alienated them further. Another teacher, whom they didn't see as a rabble rouser and whose opinion these teachers respected, talked to them about getting involved. Because she was involved, they were inspired to become involved. It is a crucial part of broadening your base of support to remember that others may sometimes be more effective in accomplishing a needed task.

Finally, work with, not against, other teachers' programs. Do not try to save your program by criticizing others. Save it positively, on its own merits.

Know Who Is Making the Decisions and Who/What Will Influence Them

You want your message going to the right people. Take the time to find out who those people are. We knew we needed to gain the support of the superintendent, the board, and the press.

In retrospect, we now realize that we underestimated the importance of middle management in shaping opinion. In many school districts, principals and program administrators serve as sounding boards for the administration or board and are in a position of giving information and advice that is taken very seriously. They may also be told to implement the board or superintendent's initiatives. If they know little about your program, they may, with no wrong intention, misrepresent your program to the board.

Think out which middle-management people you should work with in your district. There may be administrators without any direct responsibility for your program, but whose opinion district leaders strongly value. You or one of the volunteers may already know these administrators. Once responsibility for your main focus is taken, find people who can talk with influential middle-management personnel about why your program is so important.

When you arrange meetings to speak individually with decision makers, whether they are board members, the superintendent, administrators, or legislators, prepare so you can give them clear, simple information on the effectiveness of your program. Though you will be presenting your program strongly, do not make convincing this person that you are right your main goal in these meetings. Listen carefully to any questions or comments; write them down. King points out that listening is an invaluable tool that you have in opening up communication between your group and those in power. Answer questions, if you can, and then think seriously about them again later on. By asking questions and making comments, these people are telling you what you need to do to gain their support.

Find the best person to talk with each decision maker. It may be someone who knows them already, shares a common interest, is especially skilled at listening, or knows the facts of your program in great detail.

Be aware of the strengths and interests of the people to whom you are talking. Take time to think about the goals and visions of the people in power. Respect those goals, and then try to figure out how your program fits with them. Our superintendent really listens to parents. Because she truly values their opinions, we were most effective in having parents write, call, and talk to her.

If the people you want to influence are public officials, watch them in public meetings, read carefully about them in the paper, or talk with people who have worked with or against them. This homework will help you to understand them better and to find the best people to represent you— whether it is in public appearances or individual meetings.

When you speak with people or attend public hearings, pay attention to how people react to what they are hearing—it will help you to understand what matters to them. If they lean forward and listen closely to the speaker, you've got their attention. If they start ruffling through papers in front of them, you don't. If they fold their arms or start tapping their feet, they probably do not like what they are hearing. That is not necessarily a bad thing—you are trying to bring about change, and change is not always welcome.

An awareness of your listeners' reaction also helps you to know what your next step should be. The board was surprised by the number of parents who came forward to speak and who called or wrote them about Reading Recovery. Because of their reaction to the parents, we knew board members would listen to us more carefully when we met with them about the issue, or invited them to come see us teach.

No matter whose support you are trying to gain, see what affects them. For the president of our board, it seemed to be particularly the parents who spoke through interpreters. For our superintendent, it appeared to be the sheer number of parents from all over the city and all social classes who just kept on coming, meeting after meeting. Watch, at meetings, for what works.

Speak Simply and Forcefully

As a leader of your movement, you are a likely candidate to speak at hearings, meetings, or press conferences, or in individual meetings with administrators, government officials, or reporters. Preparing yourself ahead of time will help immeasurably. Preparation fosters stirring speeches and effective answers. Here are a few ideas to help you.

Giving Speeches and Testimony

Know what you want to say. You know more about your issue than other people need (or probably want) to know. Whatever your issue is, it can be summed up in one sentence. Before you think about writing a speech, clarify your issue for yourself by articulating that one sentence. Ours was the following: "The Reading Recovery cuts will keep hundreds of Madison children from learning to read."

Screenwriter and freelance writers use this technique of the one-sentence description in pitching ideas for movies and articles. To find their one sentence, they will often ask themselves the question, "What happened?" The answer to that question is their one-sentence description.

After you have refined your issue to one sentence, think of the three most important points you want to make. It is helpful to come up with a list of the seven to ten most important points first, and then hone that down to three. You will see that some points can be grouped together under one heading, and that new heading may become one of your most important points. You will also find that other points, though important, are not quite as essential as the rest. Keep working on your list until you have reduced it to the three most important points. Our three points about Reading Recovery were the following:

1. This program works.

   Research findings—nationwide, Wisconsin Third Grade Reading Test scores

   Individual examples

2. Twenty-two teachers' positions are being eliminated.

3. If the cuts go through, more than one hundred Madison children next year will be denied the instruction they need to learn to read. Each year will be one hundred more.

Having found how to describe your issue simply, you now have a framework for a talk or testimony. Use your one-sentence description as your introduction, and amplify it with your three most important points. These points will come across most powerfully if you use real-life examples. If you are defending Reading Recovery, Susan's book, *5 Kids: Stories of Children Learning to Read* may be helpful. It tells the stories of five children whose lives were changed by learning to read. You could also tell the stories of the children you have taught, changing people's names to protect their privacy, unless you have permission to use their real names. Speak from your heart.

You may also want to describe your situation with clear, simple numbers or statistics. "These cuts will keep one hundred children from learning to read next year." "Three-fourths of the children who had had Reading Recovery in first grade—children from the very bottom of their classes—passed the state third-grade reading test two years later, reading at or above average for their grade." People respond to both passionate stories from the heart and hard facts.

Conclude forcefully, defining what needs to be done about the situation and why it is important to act now. Do not omit this last part! It is not enough to describe a problem; remember to tell people what can be done about it.

You may have parents who want to come speak for you, but who have never spoken in public before and are unsure of their ability to address the school board. We did, and we were honored by their courage and commitment. They wanted to speak for us because they cared about their children and appreciated how much we had helped them.

It is crucial to support the people who are coming forward for you. One of the Reading Recovery teachers, Carol Quam, suggested to one mother that she would meet with her and help her to think out what she would say. Carol took notes, simply writing down what the mother said about how Reading Recovery had helped her son, and then helped her to fashion the notes into a one-page speech. If you are helping other people to write statements, remember to use their words and their voice, not your own. Parents will speak powerfully about their children. We offered to get the mother a translator so that she could speak in Spanish, her first language, but she refused. She herself had learned to read English by reading along silently every night as her son read to her, and she wanted to read her talk in English. The night she spoke, her husband and two children came to sit with her in the audience and listen to her speak. By being there, they felt more a part of our city and empowered in the democratic process.

When you are giving your talk, use simple words and a conversational tone. More formal speech is difficult to follow, and you want to be understood. Any media attending will be looking for sound bites or readable quotes. Sound bites grab attention, or say a lot in one or two sentences. You might want to listen several nights to the news, paying attention to clips in which an excerpt of a speech is given, to get a feel for sound bites. It might also be informative to study newspapers in your area. How are people quoted? What made what they said interesting?

Often in hearings or meetings, a time limit is placed on testimony. Find out what the limit is and do not exceed it. A double-spaced typewritten page is roughly equivalent to one minute of speaking. Use this guideline in writing, then rehearse your speech several times—in front of a friend, in front of a mirror, into a tape recorder, hiding at the back of a closet, whatever you prefer—until you are sure of its length and very familiar with its words. As you do this, you'll probably tinker a bit more. You'll say something more naturally in talking than you did in writing. You may remember a detail you really need to mention. Change your words to sound more natural and to get that detail in.

People not used to public speaking will often speak too quickly in giving a speech. It is hard to understand someone who is racing through words. We found it helpful simply to write the word *slow* at the top of every page of a talk. Without anyone knowing, we were constantly reminded to keep the right pace.

People also frequently get nervous while sitting and waiting to give a speech or to testify, perhaps wondering what questions they may be asked. It may help to bring with you an inspiring or grounding quotation to keep rereading. This can help you to remember why you are doing this and that you have the courage to do it. A few possibilities follow:

> Love, truth, and the courage to do what is right should be our . . . guideposts on this lifelong journey.
>
> CORETTA SCOTT KING (in King 1964, xx)

> Do not lose yourself in dispersion and in your surroundings. Practice mindful breathing to come back to what is happening in the present moment. Be in touch with what is wondrous, refreshing and healing both inside and around you.
>
> THICH NHAT HANH (1987, 18)

Answering Questions and Talking to Reporters

Before a public appearance, talk with someone in your group and generate a list of questions you might be asked. Come up with answers to each question. Very often, your answer can be an elaboration or restatement of one of your three main points, keeping the focus on what is important about your issue. Write the answers down with the questions, and then go over them several times, so the question and answer are firmly linked in your mind. (For some people, reading the questions and answers out loud will help them remember better.) Then, when you are asked a question, you will probably recognize it and be able to respond confidently.

Don't feel you have to answer immediately. Take a breath in and out before you speak. It will calm you and help you to focus.

If you don't know the answer to a question, you can say you don't know but will try to find out. To create a stronger impression, you can also turn the question so that it is linked to one of your three main points, and answer with one of those. Again, watch interviews on television—it is surprising how often politicians and experts do not answer the specific question they are asked, but instead respond with the point they want to make. Sometimes this is because they are so intent on answering, they haven't heard the question. Other times, it is because they know they have an important forum in the news show or interview and want to get across the most important part of their message. In other words, public exposure is limited. See it as an opportunity to give your issue publicity.

Similarly, hostile questions can work to your advantage. Reporters are trained to ask difficult or hostile questions because people will often give the best answers when they feel they are defending or explaining something that matters to them. Barbara Walters' specials are built around hostile questions asked in a caring way. People watch because the guests are usually speaking about something that is very close and important to them. A hostile question will generally get to the heart of why your issue is important. Prepare yourself ahead of time so such questions are not a surprise if they come, and use them as an opportunity to speak clearly and with conviction.

When You Didn't Do It Perfectly

You won't each time. We didn't each time. We have all thought of the better answer or the best answer a half an hour later, or falling asleep that night. Let yourself off the hook when this happens. If your better answer is really important, you can call the reporter, board member, or administrator at work the next day and say, "You know, I've thought about what you asked, and I think I can respond better." This follow-up helps to build a relationship with that person and lets her or him know that you are accessible. Offer to answer other questions and invite the interviewer to call with questions later.

What if the hostile questions come from a person who is truly antagonistic to you and to your issue, and nothing you say will ever change his mind? If you perceive most people that way, then it is probably time to reassess how you are viewing them. If it's only one or two people, a few approaches might help. Talk to a good friend about what happened, get it off your chest, and then let it go. You have more important things to do in advocating for your issue than to be angry at someone. More altruistically, follow the example of the Dalai Lama and Gandhi, and keep trying to see the hostile people in their best light. The Dalai Lama refers to the Chinese government as "my friends, the Chinese." When you can let go of anger, it is surprising how much more energy you have to focus on advancing your cause and how much more enjoyable it is.

You won't do it right each time not only in speaking, but also in political organizing. You might take comfort in the words of Martin Luther King Jr.:

> Each of us expected that set-backs would be a part of the ongoing effort. There is no tactical theory so neat that a revolutionary struggle for a share of power can be won merely by pressing a row of buttons. Human beings with all their faults and strengths constitute the mechanism of a social movement. They must make mistakes and learn from them, make more mistakes and learn anew. They must taste defeat as well as success, and discover how to live with each. Time and action are the teachers. (1964, 43)

What you are doing in standing up for public education is much more important than whether one part of your action went as well as you would have hoped. Let yourself off the hook.

Use the Language of This Political Situation

Know the principal agendas of your superintendent and board members, and address how your program accomplishes those goals. Use their language and focus because then they will be more receptive. One of our superintendent's main goals is that every child know how to read by the end of third grade. At our first board meeting teachers stood at the doors to the auditorium and distributed a handout that showed how well former Reading Recovery students scored on the Wisconsin Third Grade Reading Test. By doing this, we were framing the issue as part of the superintendent's agenda.

Most board members will have one or two main interests that either were an impetus for them to run for the board or have become their focus since being on the board. Minority achievement, accountability, standards and benchmarks, fiscal responsibility, maintaining high quality public education, and making it accessible to all are just some examples of issues that could be main interests of board members. Talk with board members and listen carefully to what they bring up and the kinds of questions they ask you. Knowing their interests will help you to speak more persuasively to each individual about the merits of your program. Keep things simple, and speak to other people's concerns.

Be a Lion

Teachers in our Reading Recovery program generally came from a background in primary education, and many primary teachers are the kind of gentle people who don't want too much attention drawn to them. This is one reason they work so well with young children—they know how to draw the focus to the child instead of to themselves.

At first blush this is not a likely pool for political activists. But almost every Reading Recovery teacher in Madison became involved politically in saving our program. Even more important, the teachers involved truly cared about our issue, and in truly caring, they were able to draw on a deeper level of courage. Here are a few thoughts that might help you find how to keep that courage with you and to inspire it in others.

High school boys on a football team for the first time are taught something very important when they are a little nervous about facing a team they think is better or stronger or more powerful: All the players on the other team put their pants on one leg at a time. That is important to remember as you stretch yourself in this political organizing, talking with powerful people, maybe doing something you have never done before. Every one of those board members, government officials, administrators, and reporters puts his pants on one leg at a time.

Saul Alinsky puts this same idea a little differently:

> So-called power institutions get away with a lot because they're not challenged. You see, power is not just what the status quo has, it is more in what we may think it has. It may have ten soldiers but if we think it has a thousand soldiers, then for all practical purposes the status quo has a thousand soldiers. Rarely do they have the power we think they have and it's amazing what happens when you just suddenly stand up and say, "Who do you think you are?" (Sanders and Alinsky 1970, 57)

George Vukelich was a well-loved writer in Madison, a kind of Northwoods Studs Terkel who spoke out for unpopular causes, and sometimes suffered difficult consequences for his stands. His radio show lost almost all its sponsors during the Vietnam War when he came out early against the war. He lost his job late in his career when he was part of a newspaper strike. He continued to stand up for what he believed in. George often said, "Don't sweat the small stuff. . . . And everything down here is small stuff." That approach has become the title of a bestseller. What you are doing in speaking up for your program and public education is right. Let that give you courage.

And don't sweat the small stuff.

When you speak individually with people whose support you are trying to gain, don't get in an argument and don't be offensive. At the same time, be careful how that instinct not to offend colors your thinking. After our first very successful board meeting, many people told us that we should stop there, that it would irritate the board if we came back again with more parents. If we had listened to that advice and gone away, the program would not have been saved.

We live in a democracy. Part of the board's responsibility as elected officials is to listen to their constituents' concerns. Don't have twenty-five speakers at every meeting, because the board will fall asleep. But if board appearances are your focus, be there again and again and again. You are not offending people; you're participating in democracy.

You will find examples of courage around you as you continue to act. Draw on that courage. Hold in your mind the image of Pa Yang, one of the refugee Southeast Asian mothers who spoke at our first board meeting. She had had very little schooling in Laos and in the Thai refugee camp where she spent years. She can't communicate easily in English, and reading English is difficult for her. It took tremendous courage for her to go to the board and speak through an interpreter, but she did it because it mattered for her children. If she can do it, we all can do it. She was a lion.

(She came and spoke at another board meeting a month later on another issue after being so successful with us. You never know the effect of the good you do. Pa Yang sees herself and her place in our country differently now.)

Look Organized and Be Organized

One of the most effective things we did at our first board meeting was to station teachers at the doors of the auditorium, handing out research findings about how Madison Reading Recovery students scored on the Wisconsin Third Grade Reading Test when they took the test two years after being in Reading Recovery. Handing out strong research made us look much more organized than we were at that point, and that was an important part of our being taken seriously. Sometimes just *looking* organized will make an impression for you.

But to keep a movement going, you can't keep flying on a wing and a prayer. You also need to *be* organized, and to do this, you need to be aware of and to rely on each other's strengths.

Write down the steps needed to accomplish your main focus. Find people to take responsibility for each step. If your number of volunteers is limited, you may need to reconsider your focus and scale it back. Find the essential, and do it.

Being organized is making well-considered decisions. Some things need to be decided immediately. Most larger strategy decisions, however, can be made one or several days after the problem comes up. After all, your first instinct may not be the best. We found it helpful to talk over a problem, come up with several ideas about how to proceed, and then *not* decide until a few days later. Letting a few days pass will often give clarity and perspective not present when you first think about a problem. Frame things, and then, when possible, give yourself the time to let things sit and forget about the issue. Your actions and thoughts will be more organized when you come back to it.

As we have said before, keep thanking people for what they do. They may end up doing more as they gain confidence and feel appreciated. If they decide not to do more, they have already made a difference.

Do It Because It's the Right Thing to Do

Don't make winning the most important thing. This may seem contrary to everything else we have said, but it's not. You may not win. When we called the first meeting of teachers, there seemed to be little chance we would save the program that year, but we knew we had to speak up for Reading Recovery. Conviction gives you strength and purpose. It is much more effective than speculation. If you are consumed with winning, you will spend a lot of energy worrying about whether or not you're going to win, and that's energy diverted from your focus.

Many of you, in addition to jobs, have children, aging parents, and other commitments in the community. Standing up for your cause because it's right will help you forge ahead, and hone your energy right where you need it.

In *The Shelter of Each Other: Rebuilding Our Families*, Mary Pipher describes her Plains grandparents, Fred and Agnes Page, and the conviction with which they lived their lives. Fred and Agnes Page always voted. Agnes was a Republican and Fred was a Democrat, and they drove into town together from the country to vote. One time they drove through a blizzard to vote, voted, and then back through the blizzard. To a modern sensibility the risks they took were foolish, because each simply cancelled the other's vote. But with their sureness in what they were doing, they possessed something difficult to find in today's more jaded era. If you do something because it's right to do it—not because you think you'll win, but just because it's right—life is simpler, and confusion falls away. Drive through the blizzard because you know you're right.

Take Care of Yourself and See Good in Life

Political organizing is very hard work. It is likely that at times you'll feel discouraged and worn out. It may be difficult to arrange child care, or ask one more time for a spouse's good offices as you run out the door to a meeting. Friends may not join you in becoming politically active, and that can be disappointing.

Remember to keep in your life whatever it is that helps you in difficult times: exercise, walking in nature, meditation, talking with a good friend, whatever it is that helps you. You may be tempted to give that up right now because you are so busy. Don't. Get enough sleep and eat well. If religion or spirituality is what gives you strength, pray or meditate while waiting for a meeting to begin. You can do this unobtrusively, with your eyes open. (You can bet King and Gandhi employed this nonviolent technique!) If prayer or meditation are not part of your life, use those first few moments before a meeting to repeat your focus to yourself, to know exactly why it is you are there. The people who are counting on you need you to find the time to remain strong.

If you have difficulties with someone, try paying attention to your breath, following it in and out. Try to see the other person and yourself with compassion. If seeing through compassion does not sound like acting politically, go back to the examples of Gandhi, King, Havel, Nhat Hanh, and the Dalai Lama.

When the action of "the fierce urgency of *now*" (King) is grounded in a recognition of beauty and goodness, it becomes self-sustaining. Gandhi, the political leader who brought the British Empire to its knees, was described by Jawaharlal Nehru like this: "His smile is delightful, his laughter infectious, and he radiates light-heartedness. There is something childlike about him which is full of charm" (Clément 1996).

Nhat Hanh, having now spent thirty years of exile in the West, continues to write of recognizing beauty, peace, and joy in life; of seeing possibility where it may not be apparent:

> In April . . . we cannot see sunflowers around Plum Village, our community in southwestern France, so you might say the sunflowers do not exist. But the local farmers have already planted thousands of seeds, and when they look to the bare hills, they see sunflowers already. The sunflowers *are there.* They lack only the conditions of sun, heat, rain and July. Just because you cannot see them does not mean that they do not exist. (Nhat Hanh 1995, 42)

King is perhaps most famous for a four-word testament to hope: "I Have a Dream." Havel, who spent years in prison for his actions, dreamed, too.

> We thought, and hence we also dreamed. We dreamed, both in and out of prison, of a Europe without barbed wire, high walls, artificially separated nations, or gigantic stockpiles of weapons, of a Europe that had done away with "blocs" . . . I am telling you of this . . . to show that it is never pointless to think about alternatives that may at the moment seem improbable, impossible or simply fantastic." (Havel 1997, 33–34).

Each of these leaders has spent dark times and confronted despair. Each has returned to the solace and power of joy and of dreaming the impossible.

Look to them for examples of seeing joy and good around you.

And you will accomplish great things.

Appendixes

Appendix A
First Meeting

March 7, 1996

Dear Reading Recovery Teachers,

With all of the changes to Reading Recovery that the Equity Formula brings, we thought it would be important to meet as Reading Recovery teachers to see how we can support the program and each other.

When:

Where (see map below):

Please come.

Douglas Street

Appendix B
Small Group Meeting Agendas

April 10 Meeting

1. Level of commitment from parents that we actually can write down

2. How to organize our April 22 meeting
   Parents
   Classroom teachers
   Former school board
   RR teachers

3. Next steps
   Coffee with school board members
   Performance/Achievement Committee or other subgroup
   of board

April 25 Meeting

1. Thank you, thank you
   Thank you to parents
   Feedback gotten

2. Next step
   Meetings:
   May 6   ??? 1–2 or more speakers
   May 20   Ask what board will do to implement?
                Kathy—forms from parents—which meeting
   June 3   Thinking regarding final meeting . . .
                (for your right brain)

3. Networking
   Angle on board members—who wants what? How to pitch?
   Start counting votes?

Appendix C
Twenty-Five Ways You Can Be Involved

To be a good citizen, you have to obey the law, you've got to go to work or be in school, you've got to pay your taxes and—oh yes—you have to serve in your community to help make it a better place.

PRESIDENT BILL CLINTON

1. Attend organizational meetings.
2. Encourage others to become involved.
3. Organize a phone tree of supporters.
4. Keep each other informed on what is happening in individual schools and areas.
5. Get parents to agree to speak at school board meetings.
6. Provide transportation for parents and children to school board meetings.
7. Arrange for translators for Limited-English-Speaking parents at school board meetings.
8. Help parents and students to prepare what they will say at school board meetings.
9. Attend school board meetings.
10. Write letters to parents.
11. Write letters to the superintendent.
12. Write letters to school board members.
13. Write letters to newspaper editors.
14. Write and send a survey to parents of present and former students.
15. Collect returned surveys to present to school board.
16. Call the school board members.
17. Call TV and radio stations.
18. Encourage parents to call school board members and the superintendent.
19. Encourage teachers in your school to call school board members and the superintendent.
20. Organize other teachers in your school to attend and to speak at school board meetings.

21. Be a liaison with specific school board members.
22. Work with your union.
23. Be creative.
24. Attend and speak at staff and committee meetings at the school and district level.
25. Provide refreshments.

Appendix D
Reading Recovery Update

Dear Reading Recovery Teachers,

Well over half of us attended the meeting on March 14th to talk about ways to save Reading Recovery as a targeted district program. We decided the most effective way we could support Reading Recovery was to ask parents of children we have taught to do two things: 1) call school board members in support of Reading Recovery, and 2) speak at the school board meetings in April, May, and June, before final funding decisions are made.

There are presently forty Reading Recovery teachers in the Madison Metropolitan School District. If we don't act to support the program now, there will be far fewer Reading Recovery teachers next year, and in a few years the program will very likely be gone, or at best, dying on the vine.

If each Reading Recovery teacher could get one or two parents and/or children to speak at the April, May, and June meetings (a total of at least six speakers), we would have almost forty to eighty speakers at each meeting! It would be a *powerful* statement in support of Reading Recovery that we think would be heard and that is quite possible for us to do.

Could you please send attached letters out to Reading Recovery parents? Feel free to change it as you wish; the form is just there to make things easier for you. Please make copies and send through the U.S. mail (not backpack mail) to your parents. Further information will be coming from the strategic planning committee. [See Appendixes G and H.]

Thanks,
Your Fellow Reading Recovery Teachers

Questions?
Call:
Barb Keresty
Kathy Levin
Patti Lucas
Susan O'Leary

Appendix E
Letter to the Superintendent

April 17, 1996

Dear Reading Recovery Staff,

Attached to this note, you will find a letter that we have written to be sent to the school board. We would like to attach a sheet to this letter listing all Reading Recovery staff members who support it. If you are *not* comfortable about having your name included on this list, please call one of us to let us know before this Friday, April 19th.

Thank you,
Sara Clark
Lisa Glueck

Reading Recovery Program Staff
Madison Metropolitan School District

Madison Metropolitan School District
Superintendent Cheryl Wilhoyte
Members of the Madison Board of Education

Dear Superintendent Wilhoyte and School Board Members:

We are writing this letter to express our concern about an inadvertent negative impact that is occurring as a result of the Madison School District's
resource allocation plan for the 1996–1997 school year. There are many positive aspects of this plan that deserve mention. The profound issue of allo-
cating resources fairly across the entire district has been a significant and
much-needed reform. On the surface, it would also seem to be a good idea
to delegate authority to individual schools to make decisions about how to
spend available funds.

Unfortunately, this freedom brings with it a shadow. Principals and
staff are forced to decide between smaller class sizes and effective supportive
programming. Naturally, classroom teachers want smaller classes. As a result,
programs such as Reading Recovery are already losing significant ground.

The Reading Recovery program began as a pilot program in Madison
in 1989. The program was selected because of its demonstrated success in
New Zealand and the United States. The investment made by the district and
the teachers involved has paid off in impressive outcomes at each school
where the program has been implemented. These successes have been
reported to the school board annually and have resulted in a gradual expansion of the Reading Recovery program.

Reading skills are fundamental to success in the educational setting and
in life. Reading Recovery is a program with a proven track record of helping
children in first grade who are at high risk of failing to learn to read. The vast
majority of these students are able to gain sufficient skills to enable them to
read within the average band in their classrooms after twenty or fewer weeks
of instruction.

The students who have attained success in the Reading Recovery program were not able to learn to read effectively in a group setting.
Traditionally, many of these students continued to experience confusion and

were eventually labeled as learning disabled. Some students do have significant learning challenges that required long-term supportive services. A significant number of these struggling first graders, however, are able to learn to read quite successfully if given intensive, individualized instruction at this crucial point in their lives. This early involvement greatly enhances the likelihood that these children will experience continued educational success.

All our students are required to attend school. It is imperative that we provide the programming they need to get off to the best possible start. If Madison is sincere in its motto of "Success for All," provision of Reading Recovery programming deserves to remain a districtwide priority.

Sincerely,

Reading Recovery Program Staff
Madison Metropolitan School District

Appendix F
Letter to the Editor

Reading Recovery Essential Program to Many Children

By Lisa Glueck and Barb Keresty

We write to express our concern about a negative effect that will occur as a result of the Madison School District's equity resource allocation plan for the 1996–97 school year.

On the surface, it would seem to be a good idea to delegate authority to individual schools to make decisions about how to use available resources. Unfortunately, this apparent freedom brings with it a dark shadow.

State-imposed revenue caps have severely limited the funds available to Madison schools despite dramatically increasing student needs. Using the district's new resource allocation process, principals and staff are forced to decide between smaller class sizes and effective supportive programming.

Most educators agree that small classes are better for learning. The result, however, is that programs such as Reading Recovery, which are also essential to the success of many children, would be sacrificed.

The Reading Recovery Program began as a pilot in Madison in 1989. The program was selected because

GUEST COLUMN

of its high level of success, supported by extensive research. The investment made by the district and the teachers involved with the Reading Recovery Program has paid off impressively at each school where the program has been implemented. These successes have been reported each year to the school board, and have resulted in a gradual expansion of the program over six years.

Reading skills are fundamental to children's success in school and in life. Reading Recovery is a program with a proven track record of helping children in first grade who are at high risk of failing to learn to read and will likely fail without this in-depth assisted learning.

After twenty or fewer weeks of instruction, the majority of these students are able to gain sufficient skills to enable them to read within the average band of their classrooms.

Students who attained success in Reading Recovery had not been able to learn to read effectively in a group setting. Prior to the availability of Reading Recovery, many of these students were confused and were labeled as learning disabled.

Some students have significant learning challenges that require long-term supportive services. A significant number of these struggling first graders, however, are able to learn quite successfully if given intensive, individualized instruction at this crucial point in their lives. This early involvement greatly enhances the likelihood these children will be successful throughout school.

Stop for a moment to reflect upon a time when everyone but you seemed to be catching on to something important. Recall your embarrassment, feeling of panic, and the tightness in your stomach? Now imagine how you would feel if that situation stretched for years into the future with no escape. Those who had "cracked the code" would appear to be so far out in front that you would eventually lose all hope of closing the gap. Then you would have a choice: Would I rather be seen as dumb or rebellious?

All students are required to attend school. It is imperative that they be provided programming which will enable them to get off to the best possible start. If Madison is sincere in its motto of "Success for all," Reading Recovery must remain a districtwide priority. The cost of this early literacy program pales in comparison to the costs of unnecessary human suffering and the possibility of more expensive long-term interventions.

Teachers and parents should not be forced to choose between programs that are essential to the well-being and success of students. This is a community that can afford to look after the needs of all students. All students deserve the best chance of success.

Glueck works at Elvehjem School and Keresty works at Van Hise School. Forty-three other Reading Recovery staffers signed on to the column.

Wisconsin State Journal, May 30, 1996

Appendix G
Form Letter for Parent Response

TO: Dr. Cheryl Wilhoyte
Members of the Madison School Board

I support keeping the Reading Recovery program in the Madison schools. I understand that the administration has not allocated any money specifically for Reading Recovery for next year.

I think that Reading Recovery should be supported by district funds and not have to come out of the individual school's "equity" budgets. When so many elementary schools have so many children with so many needs, too many schools may not have enough money for the Reading Recovery program to ensure success for all students.

I know how much Reading Recovery has helped my child, and I think that *every* child who needs it should have this chance to learn to read.

_____

Parent of a Reading Recovery Student

Developed by Kathy Levin and Joyce Dewey

Appendix H
Parent Survey

Dear Parents of _____

We are asking the parents of Reading Recovery children to think about how this program has helped their children. We want to share all of your responses with Superintendent Cheryl Wilhoyte and the Madison School Board members, so that they will know just how important Reading Recovery is to the children who need it.

Please answer the following questions, and return the paper to us in the enclosed envelope by May 28.

1. What grade is your Reading Recovery child in now?

2. Did Reading Recovery help your child?
   If so, how?

3. What kind of reader is your child?

4. What kind of writer is your child?

5. How is your Reading Recovery child doing in school now?

_____

Sign if you wish.
Thank you very much.

Appendix I
Opening Remarks to School Board

My name is Susan O'Leary, and I'm a Reading Recovery and English as a Second Language teacher at Franklin School. I am here tonight to alert the board and Dr. Wilhoyte to the damaging effect the Equity Allocation Formula will inadvertently have on Reading Recovery.

Reading Recovery, as you know, is an early intervention program for first graders at the bottom of their class. Each Reading Recovery position is a half-time allocation. We take the very, very lowest children, those who are not learning to read, and work with them one-on-one, a half hour a day, for about half a school year. At the end of their time in Reading Recovery almost all Reading Recovery students are reading at or above grade level, and they continue to do so throughout school. Reading Recovery is a dramatically effective early intervention program that quite simply changes children's lives.

The Superintendent's Equity Allocation formula is an admirable response to the budget cap imposed by the legislature on our schools. At a macro level, of course, all schools should have equal resource to teach our children as best as we possibly can. But at a micro level, this has meant that school after school has had to cut needed programs. Class size has been pitted against important programs that make class size work. Because of this, our best estimate is that the Reading Recovery program will be cut anywhere from one-third to forty percent by next year. At this rate, under the Equity Allocation Plan, the program will be gone in two years.

The micro level of individual schools having to cut programs is now back at a macro level where our neediest young students across the district will suffer the most from the Equity Allocation plan.

We currently teach over three hundred struggling first graders a year. Unless the board provides funding for the lost half-time Reading Recovery positions by making Reading Recovery a district targeted program, next year roughly 160 of Madison's six-year-olds won't have the chance to have school saved for them; won't have the chance to see themselves as bright and capable rather than as the one at the bottom of the class who can't read. Equity then has a new face. And its face is 160 first graders, across Madison, being denied the right, for years to come, to do well in school.

Reading Recovery works because we catch children before they're used to failing. We focus on their strengths—even if, as for a boy I'm teaching right now, a strength is being able to write only four words more than

halfway through first grade. We teach them strategies to become independent readers and learners. The school district paid for Dr. Hank Levin to
come to Madison last week to talk about accelerated schools. Dr. Levin, a
keynote speaker at a recent Ohio State Reading Recovery conference, supports and recommends the Reading Recovery program as being a very logi-
cal part of an accelerated school because one of the main goals of Reading
Recovery is to accelerate the lowest students' learning so they can catch up to
their peers. Both Hank Levin and Robert Slavin, director of Success for All,
conclude the lowest students need one-on-one tutoring. Reading Recovery is
the program that each of them has identified to fill this need.

Reading Recovery is cost-effective because it intervenes early in a child's
school years. We have boxes and boxes of statistics on Reading Recovery,
because every teacher daily calculates each child's percentage of words read
correctly in new text; weekly graphs the child's ability to read at what first-
grade level. Our criteria for graduation are that the child read and write at
the national average for first-grade level, using graded stanine scores. Again,
we teach the children from the very bottom of the first-grade class. In 1990,
eighty-four percent of the children we taught reached national average or
better; in 1991, eighty-four percent reached national average or better; in
1992, ninety-three percent reached national average or better; in 1993, ninety
percent; in 1994, ninety percent; in 1995, eighty-four percent.

As board members in an age of nano-statistics, you are inundated by
numbers and statistics and percentages. This is the statistic to remember
about Reading Recovery. On last year's third grade state reading test—which
obviously tested students two years after we had taught them—seventy-one
percent of students who had had Reading Recovery scored above the standard. That is close to three-fourths of the students who had been at the very
bottom of their first-grade classes—students of poverty, students from illiter-
ate homes, students from very educated upper middle-class homes who simply couldn't learn to read. Three-fourths of the very bottom of Madison's
first-grade classes scoring *above* the standard on the third-grade state reading
test after having had Reading Recovery.

Statistics are rather foreign to the way I like to see the world, which is
one student at a time, one life at a time. The parents here tonight can tell you
the one-child-at-a-time effect of Reading Recovery. One of the most common criticisms of schools asks "why Johnny can't read." Don't let the answer
to that be that the school board didn't save the reading program that would
teach him.

Listen now to the parents. Thank you.

Appendix J
Public Appearance Registration Form

Madison Metropolitan School District   Speaker #_____
Public Appearance Registration Form

Board of Education Policy 1222   Date_____

(Please print clearly)

Name_____

Street address_____

City _____ (Zip)_____

Please check the appropriate boxes:

☐ Wish to speak
☐ Do not wish to speak

Representing: ☐ Self
               ☐ Group (name)

> Please note speaking limits:
> Regular Meeting: up to 5 minutes
> Special Committees meeting: up to 3 minutes
> Public Hearing: up to 5 minutes
>
> Time may be less according to Board Policy 1222.
>
> No registrations will be accepted after a meeting has been called to order.
>
> Register 15 minutes before regular or special meeting or committee meeting, or 30 minutes before a public hearing.

Subject: _____

☐ Support   ☐ Oppose

Comments

_____
_____
_____

Appendix K
Handout for First Open School Board Meeting

Reading Recovery Program Students' Performance
on the 1995 Third-Grade Reading Test

Reading Recovery is a short-term intervention program for first graders in the bottom twenty percent of their classes. Two years after this short-term intervention:

- Seventy-one percent of Reading Recovery students scored ABOVE the standard on the third grade reading test;
- Seventy-four percent of all third-grade students, in Reading Recovery schools, who scored BELOW the standard had not received Reading Recovery instruction in first grade.

Appendix L
Response from Parents, Teachers, Principals

Some written responses about Reading Recovery from parents, teachers, and principals

From Parents:

- I only wish that every child got the opportunity to be in the program.
- This program seemed to be exactly what my son needed to keep up with his class and boost his confidence and learning.
- If this program is ever in danger of not being continued in the Madison School System, we'll be the first in the picket line at the school district's doors to battle them to the bitter end! My husband and I were both educated through Madison schools all the way from K–12 and both graduated with above-average grades, but neither of us could "get through" to our daughter to help her discover reading. This program probably saved her before it was too late!

From Classroom Teachers:

- There is no substitute for one-on-one instruction nor a "specialist." Reading Recovery has helped my students gain comprehension and fluency. Mostly, it has helped them gain self-confidence.
- I see Reading Recovery as the most effective intervention I have been involved with. I feel disappointed other children with needs could not be serviced through Reading Recovery this year. I hope we will have two Reading Recovery teachers next year.
- I am convinced that some children need one-on-one instruction in order to learn to read. Many of these children are unable to focus in small groups and certainly not in large group work.
- I feel that Reading Recovery is an *essential part of the elementary school curriculum*. The students who are involved in the program become confident readers and successful students.

From Principals:

- Reduced number of students experiencing failure in reading.
- We don't have Title I, it has allowed us to *avoid* several retentions and probable special education placements.
- We are using some consistent language with students, attaining some consistent methodologies, and introducing and integrating the same in regular classroom.
- Reading instruction has changed as a result of the program, more coordination between classroom teachers and Reading Recovery Teachers.

Appendix M
Instruction for Participation at School Board Meetings

DATE: 4/11/96
TO: Reading Recovery Teachers
RE: Speakers for the Reading Recovery Program at the Board Meeting on April 22, 1996, 6:45 p.m.

In order to facilitate a smooth presentation at the board meeting on Monday evening, April 22, you are asked to do the following:

1. Submit name and address of person(s) speaking for Reading Recovery to Barb Keresty, ATM, Rm. 117, administration building or drop off at her home, _____, by Thursday, April 18, at the latest.
2. Make sure that you tell anyone planning on attending the meeting, but not speaking, to be sure to fill out the form at the front of the auditorium, registering their written support.
3. Send any parent surveys that may have been returned to you to Kathy Levin. (Not all of you will have done this, but if you did send home the survey, send returns to Kathy.)

Some additional information you should know:

1. Anyone planning on speaking must have a registration form. Once we have the names and addresses of those planning on speaking, we will fill out the forms for them. They will be together in a packet so that all our speakers can follow one another.
2. Speakers should sit as close to the front of the auditorium as possible so they can get up to the podium as quickly as possible.
3. Speakers should limit "speech" to three minutes.

Good luck in getting out the supporters (as many teachers, parents, and children as possible). They don't all have to speak.

Return by Thursday, 4/18/96, to Barb Keresty, ATM, Rm. 117 or _____.

- -

Speaker's Name: _____

Address: _____

_____

_____

Appendix N
MTI Voters School Board Election Questionnaire

MTI VOTERS
1996 School Board Election Questionnaire

On separate paper, please address each of the following questions by numbering your responses in the same sequence as the questions.

1. Summarize your qualifications to serve on the board of education of the Madison Metropolitan School District (MMSD).
2. Explain why you are running for the seat that you have designated.
3. Identify the priorities you would bring to the board should you be (re)elected.
4. Identify specific MMSD programs and/or policies that you believe need to be modified, reprioritized, or eliminated.
5. Describe your views on
   a. construction of an Allied Drive area school
   b. the Midvale/Lincoln and Franklin/Randall paired schools
   c. proposed attendance options for West/Memorial area K–8 students
   d. integration, neighborhood schools, busing, and other educational strategies
6. Discuss your views on the East Area Study Committee Recommendations.
7. Discuss the strengths and weaknesses of the "Madison Schools 2000" strategic plan. Discuss your willingness to finance the recommendations.
8. Explain your general philosophy about bond referenda. Apply that thinking to 5-a and 6 above.
9. Do you support the recommendations of the 1995 MMSD Blue Ribbon Panel Report to fund recurring maintenance expenditures in the operating budget? If yes, identify the seven million dollar annual expenditures that you will eliminate.
10. Summarize your thoughts about the performance of Superintendent Wilhoyte.
11. What should the district be doing to reduce violence in our schools?

12. Explain any concerns/solutions you have about the district's minority achievement efforts.

13. Explain your commitment to four-year-old and all-day kindergarten programs.

14. Should elementary teacher planning time be increased? If yes, how could this be accomplished?

15. Discuss the problems, if any, you see with nonadministrative staff (teachers, support staff, etc.) participating in management decisions (for example, site-based management).

16. Summarize your thoughts about the recent reorganization of the Integrated Student Services and the Curriculum and Instruction Departments. Do you support the current Equity/Diversity/Advocacy Department? Why?

17. Describe your perspective about including "alternative families" in district curricula and in employee benefit packages. Should the Equity/Diversity/Advocacy Department become involved with "alternative family" issues?

18. Do you believe there is less public input/access to the board because the number of televised meetings has been decreased?

19. From what sources should public schools be funded?

20. Summarize your thinking about the state imposed "caps."

21. Do you support the movement to decrease class size K–1 to 15:1 and increase class size to 23.5:1 for grades 2–5 at Chapter/Title I schools?

22. Do you support the expansion of charter schools in the district? Why?

23. Do you support the concept of school choice? Inter and/or intra public school district choice? Public funds for private school choice? Do you support:
    a. the use of vouchers to transfer to private/parochial schools the property taxes that were collected to fund public schools?
    b. providing parents the "choice" to give their children the option of attending any school within their school district?
    c. providing parents the "choice" to give their children the option of attending school in another school district?

24. For your campaign, are you accepting political action contributions? If so, from which groups do you expect funding?

25. Identify MMSD teaching and/or management staff from whom you seek advice. What previous or current board member do you most admire? Why?

26. Have you ever had any of your children enrolled in MMSD schools? If yes, which schools and when?

27. Have you ever had any of your children enrolled in a private/parochial school (K–12)?

28. If you have ever been employed as a teacher, please describe why you decided to leave the teaching profession.

29. Do you support the inclusion instruction model for including Title I, EEN, and ESL students in the regular classroom?

Appendix O
Press Release

For More Information Contact:
Dale Wortley, Ph.D.   Barb Keresty   Susan O'Leary   Marlys Sloup

For immediate release—May 28, 1996

Abandoning First Graders to Failure

Investment in Reading Recovery Saves District Dollars; Children's Self-Esteem

In the 1995–1996 school year, more than one-third of Madison's least skilled first-grade readers did not get the help needed to master the most essential of the R's—Reading. With more cuts destined for the 1996–1997 school year budget, even more children will be at risk for not attaining an average reading level by the time they graduate from first grade. This despite the fact that a proven, successful district program called Reading Recovery could be made more readily available.

The children in need come from all socioeconomic backgrounds and are equally deserving of the opportunity to learn how to read. "Reading is probably the best antipoverty program we have," says Barb Keresty, Reading Recovery teacher. "It is critical to success in any income group." To ensure that all children who would benefit by this program have access, Reading Recovery must be established as a targeted district program.

"There is nothing more important in all of education and our community than the ability to read and write. It's connected directly to the ability to reason, to communicate, and to become a meaningful contributor to society. As a matter of fact, the inability to read is directly correlated to increased delinquency, antisocial behavior, low self-esteem, and a decreased ability to earn a living wage," says Keresty.

"It's important to focus on savings, but it's hard to overstate the value of a child's self-esteem. Investing in teaching children how to read will be paid back manifold by their participation in all aspects of school and community life."

Reading Recovery is an early, short-term intervention system designed for first graders at risk of failing to learn to read. Reading Recovery focuses on early intervention, the benefits of which have been noted by educators for years. Investing money early to nip problems in the making is regarded as the best way to avoid costly remedial programs and to guarantee success in later years at school.

In the Reading Recovery program specially trained teachers provide high-quality, research-supported, individual instruction *that allows students to succeed before they enter a cycle of failure.* Children are expected to make faster-than-average progress so they can catch up with their peers and lose little regular class time.

Reading Recovery has a rigorous research design that continuously monitors program results and provides support to participating teachers and institutions. Data are collected on all students who participate in the program. Testing scores on the national level are mirrored locally:

- Approximately seventy to eighty percent of the lowest twenty percent of children served by Reading Recovery have achieved reading and writing scores in at least the average range of their classes and received no additional supplemental instruction.
- The progress in reading and writing is sustained and the students' performance in the average band has been measured up to three years after the children graduated from the program.
- Studies have shown Reading Recovery to be more effective in achieving short-term and sustained progress in reading and writing than other intervention programs.
- Reading Recovery has been found to be cost-effective when compared to remedial reading programs, special education placement, and primary grade retention.

Prepared by Mae Knowles

Appendix P
Prepared Talk for Press Conference

We are here today to speak for the six-year-olds who are failing in school. Reading Recovery is a program that can save them. Reading Recovery is an early intervention program that takes children from the bottom of their first-grade classes and advances them to the middle in about a semester's time. The Reading Recovery program, proven over and over again to succeed, has been cut in half for next year's budget.

Because six-year-olds can't call press conferences, we are here to speak for the children and to save their Reading Recovery program. Our children have a right to learn to read and we have the responsibility to teach them.

The school budget is tight and hard choices have to be made. But what in the budget is more important than our lowest readers learning to read? Reading Recovery has been proven year after year to succeed. There is no risk in putting our time and money into Reading Recovery because we know it works.

What is the cost if we don't teach children to read? National studies show a high correlation between nonreaders and teenage pregnancies, crime, and high school dropout rates. Reading Recovery is cost-effective because it is an investment in the rest of a child's education and in our community. Anyone can have a child who can't read. Parents of nonreaders span the economic spectrum. We call on the school board to restore the cuts in the budget and establish Reading Recovery as a targeted program.

Appendix Q
Headline News

Campaign Aims to Save Reading Recovery Program

One-on-One Instruction for Children Who Fall Behind in Reading Skills
Monday, May 20, 1996
By Phil Brinkman, Education Reporter

With his mother propping him up on the lectern, 6-year-old Quinn Felly read clearly into the microphone, "Once upon a time a boy had three goats."

He was reading a story to the Madison School Board. But the real story was Quinn's own: Just six months ago, his mother said, Quinn couldn't read past the word *the*.

Now, thanks to the district's intensive reading recovery program, the Thoreau Elementary first-grader can keep up with the rest of his class.

"He wasn't into anything," his mom, Holly Felly, said. "They took him for twenty minutes a day and turned his life around."

The demonstration, and others like it, are part of an ongoing campaign by teachers and parents to persuade the board to restore funding to the program, an early flash point in Superintendent Cheryl Wilhoyte's proposed $222.9 million budget for next year.

Supporters plan to continue their push at public hearings at 7 p.m. today at Cherokee Middle School and 7 p.m. Tuesday at LaFollette High School.

Introduced in the district seven years ago, Reading Recovery gives teachers a chance to provide one-on-one instruction with up to four students a semester. Begun with thirty-seven students, the program enrolls more than 250 today.

It combines reading stories and using picture books to help children decipher words—commonly known as whole language instruction—with some elements of phonics.

While Wilhoyte's budget doesn't actually cut Reading Recovery teachers, the roughly forty half-time teachers will no longer be funded separately from a school's total teacher allocation.

Instead, schools will be given a set number of teaching positions to use as they wish. That means principals can choose to keep programs such as Reading Recovery and talented and gifted programs, district spokesman Mike McCabe said. Or they can use them in other ways, including putting them in regular classrooms to lower class sizes.

"If you look at the total pie, the pie is no different than it was,"

McCabe said. "What this does is give schools the flexibility to decide whether Reading Recovery is the best delivery mechanism."

Advocates of the program say that isn't enough. Some fear that principals, under pressure to keep class sizes small, won't see the value in preserving such a labor-intensive program. To see the full effects of the program, they say, it needs to be maintained on a districtwide scale.

"I don't care how small the class is, or how good the teacher is, there are a certain number of your lowest two, three or four kids who still aren't going to make the progress they need to keep up with their peers," said Dale Wortley, a Reading Recovery teacher and teacher trainer.

There is evidence the program works. Last year, 71 percent of the students who went through the program as first graders performed above the state standard on the third grade reading test. The year before, 72 percent did.

There is also evidence it is needed. Madison's third graders as a whole consistently score below the state average on the third grade reading test, the only important state measure where the district does not excel.

Erik Heimark, a first grader at Van Hise Elementary, is close to graduating from the program. When he started this winter, he, too, could recognize only the word *the* on a diagnostic test. On a recent morning he read enthusiastically from a small book about "Mrs. Pig and her marshmallow necklace," his finger tracing his progress.

Stumbling only occasionally, he reads: "Mrs. Pig wants her friends to come to a party let's." His teacher, Barbara Keresty, asks him if that makes sense. He agrees it doesn't, and goes back over the line, this time reading correctly: "Mrs. Pig wants her friends to come to a picnic lunch."

Because the new allocation formula gives extra teachers to schools with more poor children, district officials say those schools are more likely to be able to continue the program.

But anyone can have a child with reading difficulties, Keresty said. She is worried that at some schools, which don't otherwise qualify for federal reading assistance due to numbers of poor children, slow readers will fall through the cracks.

Elvehjem Elementary, 5106 Academy Drive, is one such school. Under the new teacher allocation formula, it is slated to lose the equivalent of 3.5 full-time teachers, more than any other school.

Nevertheless, Principal Jane Belmore said she is committed to keeping Reading Recovery, although she'll have to pare it back from two half-time teachers this year to one next year. And there will be another price.

"We've had to make the decision to go with substantially larger class sizes in first grade" to keep the program, Belmore said.

While the allocation formula provides for one first-grade teacher for each twenty-two students, keeping Reading Recovery will require class sizes of twenty-five students, Belmore said.

Wilhoyte's budget calls for giving schools $400,000 next year to incorporate specialized instruction, such as Reading Recovery and talented and gifted programs, into their regular curriculum.

1996 Madison Newspapers, Inc.

State Journal photo/L. Roger Turner

Reading recovery teacher Barbara Keresty reviews a word with Van Hise first grader Erik Heimark. Such individualized instruction has helped move Erik in about four months from a nonreader to one who can keep up with his peers.

Appendix R
Dear Teachers and Parents

Dear Teachers and Parents,

Reading Recovery has now been cut in half districtwide. *In the next two weeks*, we need you to call these board members and tell them that you want Reading Recovery to be a district targeted program (this means it would be a part of the operational budget, and not subject to cuts each year), so that we can be sure it's available for all the kids who need it.

We need four members' votes to make Reading Recovery a targeted program. The board has been impressed by all the speakers at the board meetings. With your phone calls, we can get the votes we need.

Please concentrate on these board members (list names, phone numbers, and e-mail addresses):

Names and what will convince them:

Thank you for your support!

Appendix S
Quotation from *No Quick Fix*

While the conventional wisdom has often recommended slowing instruction down, there is an alternative that involves accelerating the instruction offered. Acceleration of instruction means that we offer children larger amounts of more intense teaching in order to enhance the pace of literacy development . . . Children who begin school with fewer experiences with literacy need not remain behind their more advantaged peers throughout their school careers. In fact, designing schools that offer instruction that accelerates development early, in kindergarten and first grade, must become our priority. The longer we allow children's development to lag behind that of their peers, the more difficult it becomes to accelerate their learning and the less likely it is that these children will ever develop full literacy. (8)

Allington, Richard L., and Sean A. Walmsley, eds. 1995. *No Quick Fix: Rethinking Literacy Programs in America's Elementary Schools.* New York: Teachers College Press.

Appendix T
Quotation from *Partners in Learning*

Children's success in school depends on quality education from the start. Amid public concerns about education in general, many researchers have turned their attention to the early experience children have in school. Here, becoming literate is a priority. It is every child's right to receive the needed level of support to be successful in their early literacy experiences and continue that success throughout their years of schooling. Meeting the needs of a diverse population of students is a challenge for educators, one that must be met if we are to maintain the quality of life of our citizens. For many children, we need to do it better. And teachers are the key to making that happen. (xv)

Lyons, Carol A., Gay Su Pinnell, and Diane E. DeFord 1993. *Partners in Learning.* New York: Teachers College Press.

Bibliography

The following are a few books by or about the political and educational leaders we have cited. These books should lead you to a more extensive bibliography for each author.

Alinsky, Saul. 1946. *Reveille for Radicals*. New York: Random House.

———. 1971. *Rules for Radicals*. New York: Random House.

Allington, Richard, and Sean A. Walmsley. 1995. *No Quick Fix: Rethinking Literacy Programs in America's Elementary Schools*. New York: Teachers College Press.

Clay, Marie. 1983. *The Early Detection of Reading Difficulties*. Portsmouth, NH: Heinemann.

———. 1994. *Literacy, Teaching, and Learning*. 1 (1). San Bernardino, CA: California State University.

Clément, Catherine. 1996. *Gandhi, The Power of Pacifism*. New York: Henry Abrams.

Gandhi, Mahatma. 1982. *The Words of Gandhi*. Edited by Richard Attenborough. New York: Newmarket Press.

———. 1991. *The Essential Writings of Mahatma Gandhi*. Edited by Raghavan Iyer. Delhi: Oxford University Press.

Havel, Václav. 1997. *The Art of the Impossible: Politics as Morality in Practice*. Translated by Paul Wilson et al. New York: Alfred A. Knopf.

King, Martin Luther, Jr. 1964. *Why We Can't Wait*. New York: Mentor.

———. 1987. *The Words of Martin Luther King, Jr*. New York: Newmarket Press.

Lyons, Carol A., Gay Su Pinnell, and Diane E. DeFord. 1993. *Partners in Learning*. New York: Teachers College Press.

Matthews, John. 1997. Speech presented to the Wisconsin Education Association Council Election 1997 Work Group, Madison, WI, January 13.

Nhat Hanh, Thich. 1975. *The Miracle of Mindfulness: A Manual on Meditation.* Boston: Beacon Press.

———. 1987. *Interbeing: Fourteen Guidelines for Engaged Buddhism.* Berkeley: Parallax Press.

———. 1991. *Peace Is Every Step: The Path of Mindfulness in Everyday Life.* New York: Bantam Press.

———. 1993. *Love in Action: Writings on Nonviolent Social Action.* Berkeley: Parallax Press.

———. 1995. *Living Buddha, Living Christ.* New York: G. P. Putnam.

O'Leary, Susan. 1997. *5 Kids: Stories of Children Learning to Read.* Bothell, WA: The Wright Group.

Pipher, Mary. 1996. *The Shelter of Each Other: Rebuilding Our Families.* New York: Putnam.

Routman, Regie. 1996. *Literacy at the Crossroads: Crucial Talk About Reading, Writing, and Other Teaching Dilemmas.* Portsmouth, NH: Heinemann.

Sanders, Marion K., and Saul Alinsky. 1970. *The Professional Radical: Conversations with Saul Alinsky.* New York: Harper & Row.

Websites

For information on the political writings of Thomas Jefferson:
http://etext.virginia.edu/jefferson/quotations/jeff1370.htm
(See especially sections 38 and 39.)

For information on Martin Luther King Jr:
http://www-leland.stanford.edu/group/king/KCenter/kcenter.htm#top

For information on Thich Nhat Hanh:
http://www.parallax.org